SPUR PUBLICATIONS

EXHIBITION AND FAMILY PETS SERIES

BOOK OF THE NETHERLAND DWARF

Book of the

Netherland Dwarf

by

DENISE CUMPSTY, S.R.N., L.R.A.M.

PUBLISHED BY SPUR PUBLICATIONS
SAIGA PUBLISHING CO LTD
1 ROYAL PARADE, HINDHEAD
SURREY, GU26 6TD, ENGLAND

ISBN 0 904558 45 2

Typeset by Inforum, Portsmouth
Printed and bound by
The Pitman Press, Bath

Published by
SAIGA PUBLISHING CO LTD
1 ROYAL PARADE
HINDHEAD, SURREY

Contents

Introduction

You, the reader, have the right to ask what authority have I for writing this book. If you are not particularly interested in this aspect, pass straight on to Chapter 1.

I have bred and exhibited Netherland Dwarfs, Beverens and Satins in every available shade up to this date, and Polish in Smoke Pearl, Sable, Red eyed and Blue eyed Whites.

I have won every award of consequence in the first three breeds as well as awards in Polish. These have been won at Major Shows. I have judged at all Major Shows on many occasions and I am on many National Specialist Club Panels, including that of the Netherland Dwarf. I have been breeding Dwarfs for 22 years, and I have bred and shown dogs in my earlier days and bred cats for nearly as long.

Confines of this Book

I shall confine myself to covering only things that concern the Netherland Dwarf. There are many excellent books already available on the general aspects of rabbits. These are *not* **what the Dwarf breeder needs, as the requirements for the Netherland Dwarf are often different and are, therefore, quite specific to the breed. Only a Dwarf breeder truly understands this. Many people make the mistake of thinking that a general book on such things as housing, feeding methods; etc. will cover the Dwarf equally. It will NOT. So, I have tried to put everything the beginner needs to know into one book.**

The 'Making' of the Netherland Dwarf

The Netherland Dwarf is a 'made' breed. There are several ways in which a breed comes about, as opposed to 'just a rabbit' and there are good books on this subject alone. We will concern ourselves, very briefly, with what appertains to the Netherland Dwarf.

It came about by a combination of two methods, described now in basic form. Fanciers interested in Genetics can obtain books on loan from the British Rabbit Council's library, or buy them from various publishers advertising frequently in *Fur & Feather*, if they wish.

In horticulture, if a plant produces something totally different from the flowers or leaves on the parent plant, it is called a 'sport' or mutation. This is how new colours and species are discovered, 'dwarfing' being a common one found. Something 'odd' turns up, someone sees possibilities and spends years in developing, experimenting, selecting, and recording results, until this phenomenon can be produced at will. (What is called 'breeding true'.) That person then has a new species. Roughly speaking, this is how Netherland Dwarfs came about.

Origins

They originated in England in the 'sport' stage. A few breeders of Dutch rabbits found some white selfs appearing in their litters. They were no use to them, and were usually cast out. Some had red eyes and eventually, a few enterprising breeders began breeding them together, in exactly the way an horticulturist does with his plants. Most of these Dutch 'sports' went abroad to the continent, where their possibilities were seen and a great deal of work and enthusiasm produced what eventually became our Netherland Dwarf.

Recording Results

For such an enterprise to succeed, strict records must be kept, and with our present standard of knowledge of genetics, one can make a good prognosis of what will turn up, and in what proportions in litters. It does, however, involve keeping every animal bred.

If you are really interested in the actual development of the Netherland Dwarf and how it all came about, there is a first class book written by a Dutchman entitled *Het Gekleurde Pwerk Gonion*, by Verhelst and Vermeulin. This is a very detailed account although written in Dutch.

That is all I propose to say on how the Netherland Dwarf came about, except to reiterate, that it was by (a) the recognition of a 'sport' and its possibilities, and (b) the breeding together of animals showing these characteristics, that the experimental breeders produced, eventually, a new breed.

Genetics

You will need some basic knowledge of this, unless you are one of those breeders who have an instinctive flair for pairing up the right animals. Many of the old breeders had it; but, alas, with our highly technical age, this instinct may well disappear.

In the ensuing chapters, most of you will learn the basic principles easily and painlessly as you go along. Following the methods set out, you will be automatically following a genetical procedure. To breed consistently good stock this is essential.

For more advanced knowledge, if you become interested and wish to experiment there are many books to suit varying stages of progress.

Acknowledgements

I am greatly indebted to all those who have helped me with this book, and should like to thank Mr. Len Askew of Portsmouth, who has done the drawings, Mr. Ian Mumford of Spennymoor, Co. Durham, who is responsible for the scale drawings, and Mr. Ken Walker, who painted the pictures in the chapter on wild flowers.

I feel that mention should also be made of Mr. Martin Wood of Ilford, who is a professional photographer as well as Dwarf fancier, and who kindly took a large number of pictures for me, which were unfortunately stolen, along with his expensive equipment, before he could get them to me. This was a serious loss for us both.

The chapter 'How to reach the Top and Stay There' is based almost completely on an article written for 'Fur & Feather' some time ago and I am grateful for their permission to use it.

Portsmouth   DENISE CUMPSTY

CHAPTER 1

Why the Netherland Dwarf?

THE FASCINATION

What is it about the Netherland Dwarf that makes it so fascinating?

First, it has all the undeniable attraction of the miniature. Like a small child, it is appealing and vulnerable. Unlike a Dwarf in real life, it is not deformed, but is perfectly normal in all respects except size.

The miniature animal has always had an attraction for some people. This is particularly true in the dog world. Miniatures are big business in Art circles. Even the motor trade has its 'minis'.

VARIETY OF COLOURS

Is it the availability in so many colours, that has attracted you? In these days, the Dwarf can be found in about every colour, as well as variety of pattern. Some are more advanced than others. Some still need a good deal of work. Does this appeal?

CHARACTER

Perhaps you have liked it for its character. It has plenty of this. It is sturdy, independent, highly individual and entertaining. It is, like the Polish, a natural showman. It can be trained to show off its good points; but, because of its very independence, it requires a lot of patience. A Dwarf can be trained to show itself to such advantage that, on occasions, it can sometimes beat a basically better exhibit, which consistently refuses to 'show' properly. As, for example, one that continually crosses its ears, 'puts them flat', or 'sits long', no matter how many times the judge tries to make it perform better.

1

There will be more about this in the chapter on Training the Show Specimen.

Do *not* fall into the trap of thinking it is a gentle pretty pet. It is *not*. It is capable of giving a very nasty bite. One of the worst bites I have ever received was from a Netherland Dwarf, and I carry the scar to this day, twenty years later. Never let a Juvenile start with Dwarfs until accustomed to something larger and more predictable.

SPACE

A major factor in choice may have had to be how much space for hutches was available. One can keep four Dwarfs in the space needed for one Beveren or one Flemish Giant or one New Zealand White. (Each of these will probably consume roughly the same amount of food as four Dwarfs, another point worth considering.)

To succeed in breeding show stock, it will be necessary to keep a number of animals. Some will be at their Show stage, some will be breeding, others will be resting. Others will be youngsters, not yet old enough for decisions on which are to be kept and which discarded.

More than one stud buck will be required as you progress, bucks excelling in certain qualities you wish to imprint on your stock. One buck will not possess them all. You will certainly have at least three bucks in regular use. It is worth keeping a buck that continually produces a particular feature, wanted or needed, for that one thing alone.

If some does are weak in certain qualities, a buck particularly strong in that point will be a necessity. In this way, you will weed out undesirable characteristics and imprint and improve others. You will be choosing and selecting. In this way, also, you will be building up your own individual strain, the final achievement for which all strive. To be able to look along a table of exhibits and recognise your own, or see someone else look along a table and say, 'That's one of so and so's, for sure', is worth waiting and striving for. It sets the seal on a stud, proclaiming years of hard work and dedication.

EXPENSE

A large factor has to be cost. There are many aspects to this.

Feeding

Things to consider will have been (a) What form of feeding do you wish to use? (b) What forms of foodstuffs are easily obtainable?

2

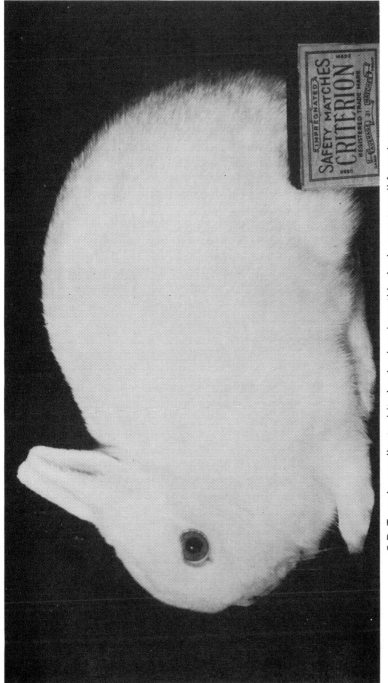

C.R. Teare's excellent white buck, showing cobby body, erect, well furred ears with rounded tips, bold eye, equidistant between eye to nose and eye to roots of ear and "roman" nose.
Note: matchbox alongside to denote size.

In the cities and towns, there may not be much choice but to buy. It is possible that you may have a friend in some related trade, pet shop, commercial meat association selling grain, a corn chandler, etc.

If not, you may find your local Fur and Feather Club has a bulk buying scheme for its members. Join this Club, because you are going to need all the help they can give you, and it is where your show career will begin. You may be able to get someone else interested in sharing the costs of buying larger quantities with you.

It is worth remembering that you get a reasonable discount for taking a hundredweight, or even half a hundredweight, in the towns. Some wholesalers and distributors will give another small discount, too, if you collect it yourself. These concessions can make a big difference to your bill over a whole year. Do try to get your food from wholesalers rather than small shops.

If you live in the country or a village, you may know a farmer who will be willing to sell you a sack of oats or bale of hay or straw, much cheaper than you would pay in town.

A good selection of wildfood is ready to hand, free, in the country. In the towns, there are local markets to consider, or a friendly greengrocer.

Cost of Show Travelling

For Shows, you will have thought about how to get your stock there and back. By rail, four Dwarfs in one multi carry box, will cost roughly what one of the larger breeds will in rail fares. If you intend to go in your own transport, you can ignore this problem, of course. But if you are asking friends for help (today's usual method), a small Dwarf can be tucked in, where a big box would be out of the question. Conversely, if a bigger box IS acceptable, then you have the chance to send more rabbits in the same space.

Final Decision

When all these questions have been satisfactorily answered, you will have to whittle down the possible choice of breeds, and it becomes purely a matter of personal preference. You would be foolish not to consider all these points, you could end up with a lot of trouble in the future and heartbreak.

On all the major counts, the Netherland Dwarf fills the bill admirably.

4

Comparative size of the Adult Dwarf
with normal breeds of 6-8 lbs

INDEX

Use the index. You will find some things repeated in several chapters in this book, because they are related to more than one aspect. The index will tell you where to find what you need.

The book is intended for beginners, or the less experienced, but others may find something of interest.

READING THE BOOK

It might be wise to read the whole of this book through first, even if only superficially, before launching out in the purchase of stock, housing, feeding stuffs. A fair idea of what is covered in it will have been gained, and possibly money saved. Then go back at leisure, reading such parts or chapters as required.

You have chosen the Netherland Dwarf. A good choice. I hope you are going to have many years of fun and happiness ahead of you.

So, let us now get on to the business of breeding and rearing winners.

CHAPTER 2

Hutches

ENOUGH SPACE VITAL

Don't make the mistake of thinking because you have a small rabbit, you can keep it in a small hutch. A Dwarf needs space in which to move about, if it is to avoid getting sore and bare patches under its feet and pads.

Its ears will grow long, it **must** have height. One of the surest ways of making a rabbit's ears grow, is to put it in a hutch with a low ceiling. The lack of air and the warmth generated will cause the ears to grow and, eventually, to lop over.

SUITABLE SIZES

Aim for hutches 20 inches high, by 20 inches deep, by 18 to 20 inches long. *Fur and Feather* advertise splendid hutches suitable for Dwarf use, many with divisions that can be removed for breeding and then put back, when the young need separating. Sydenham Hannaford Ltd. of Hamworthy Junction, Poole, Dorset, make some excellent cavy hutches, that are particularly good for three- and four-month-old youngsters, which show possibilities of making up well, and need separating, but which would find a full size hutch cold and frightening. Plenty of **AIR** and **HEIGHT** are **ESSENTIALS**.

BEDDING

This is not always easy to find. There are various methods, and it is mainly a matter of personal choice and, again, availability.

You must have sufficient depth of something absorbent to soak up the urine. Sawdust is ideal. It needs to be not less than ½ inch deep.

7

On top should be something that allows the wet to drain through, but which will dry out fairly quickly. Hay is expensive and can be scarce; but a Dwarf is not a large creature and requires only about a quarter the amount used by other breeds, so it is really worth the expense. Straw can so easily poke into the eye, especially if they burrow in or under it.

Some breeders favour shavings. These are usually much easier to obtain; but, if you do decide on them, make sure they are from soft woods.

FRONT MESH

Be sure to use a good wire mesh for the fronts. Wire netting is not desirable and simply will not do. Use one of the very good welded varieties, which are advertised in *Fur and Feather* and many animal trade magazines. Mice and flies very easily get through cheap netting and spread disease and irritation. It easily rusts, also, and needs replacing frequently. It does not remain taut, but sags and bulges.

LITTER BOARDS

It is absolutely essential to have litter boards. These prevent the rabbits — especially the babies, as well as the bedding — from tumbling out, when doors are opened. They should drop into slots on either side to allow of easy removal for cleaning out purposes. They are needed in both day and night quarters. They need to be painted on both sides, when painting the hutches, to prevent them deteriorating with wet from weather and urine.

ADVANTAGES OF MAKING YOUR OWN HUTCH

This can be cheaper, of course, and has a number of advantages, but it is better not attempted if you are not a handyman. Unless you are really sure of what you are doing, then it will be better and cheaper, in the long run, to buy.

The biggest advantage is that you can incorporate all the points you like, from those you have seen, into one hutch.

Hutches can be constructed of a variety of things. Auction sales and Jumble sales are sources of chests of drawers and wardrobes, tables, etc., made of good solid wood.

All wood should be tongued and grooved and the floors of at least ½ inch thickness. Sleeping compartments can be separated from day quarters and made of solid wood, with space left at the back for the rabbits to run in and out of the two compartments. This also provides somewhere for them to shelter from the rain and wind.

SHUTTERS

Shutters can be provided for the fronts, although they may add weight to the hinges. Leave a space at the top for ventilation. Separate ones for each hutch are best, if possible. You may want to cover up just one rabbit for some special reason.

If you are only going to make one general cover for a tier of hutches, there is an easy and inexpensive way of doing it, that even the most hamfisted of amateurs can manage.

All that is needed is a large wooden frame to fit all over the outer front compartments. Onto this, fix good quality roofing felt. Tack it well and securely on all round the frame. Attach brass rings to each of the four corners. Screw brass cup hooks into each of the four corners of the hutch front (not forgetting to position them by holding your frame up against the hutch). Remember that you will have to turn your bottom cup hooks **up** when hanging the shutter, then when it is safely hanging on the top two hooks, you turn the bottom two down, through the rings. This makes quite a good protector and because it does not fit tautly, it allows sufficient air to get through. Paint your frames and felt with black bitumastic paint, of the quick dry variety and it will be waterproof for a long time. It is easily and quickly put up and taken down.

Covers are not needed in indoor rabbitries, of course. The latter are more pleasant for the fancier and are warm and dry for the stock, also; but an outdoor rabbit grows a thicker coat and is hardier.

EXPOSURE TO SUNLIGHT

Care must be taken to see that direct sunlight is excluded, which, apart from heat, can affect the colour of the coat.

HINGES

Use brass hinges, if you can afford it, they will last for years. A

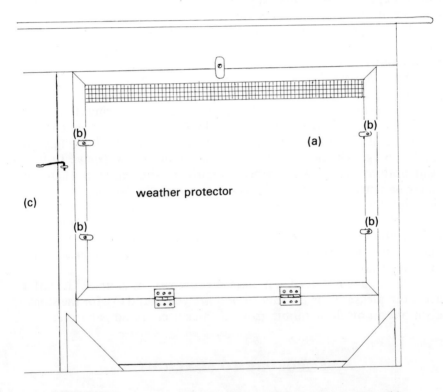

The weather protector (a) is held in position by turn buttons (b)
(c) breeding compartment

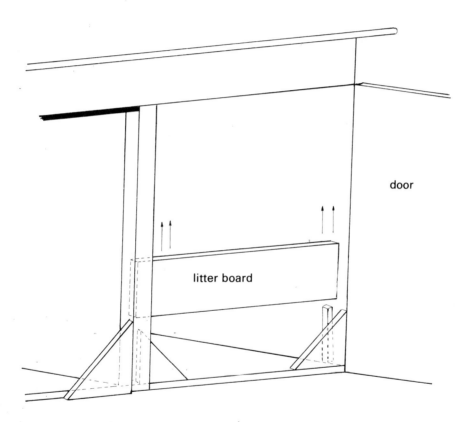

door

litter board

To remove the litter board from the breeding compartment in order to clean out soiled bedding, lift the board in the direction of the double arrows.

home-made hinge can be quite satisfactory, however. Use some pieces of leather (straps are ideal). Cut them into squares or oblongs and nail them securely to the doors and the hutch frames. Remember that the doors may tend to 'hang' when opened, so be sure the leather is of a sufficient thickness to support the weight.

WATERPROOFING

Roofing felt will protect the roof adequately, making sure there is plenty of overhang back and front; also that the top slopes away towards the back to allow the rain to run off, if the hutches are outside.

Allow a good space at the back for the circulation of air or you will end up with sodden and rotten backs.

Black bitumastic paint of the quick drying variety mentioned earlier will waterproof the floors as well as the roofing felt. (The coloured bitumastic paint is a lot more expensive.) Be absolutely sure you get the quick drying kind which will dry in about four hours, making floors quite ready for stock to be put in. This also prevents seepage of urine through the wooden floors to the hutch below. The painting can be done very quickly, as for instance if a rabbit has died or been ill in a hutch, and disinfection is required.

It can be used on the outsides as well if you wish. However, creosote is very commonly used and perfectly adequate, although you will have this chore to do every year, in that case. You **can** creosote the insides if you wish, but creosote is poisonous stuff, and, if used inside, allow at least two whole days for it to dry out thoroughly. Whitewash is much to be preferred for inside painting, in my opinion; but you will have to decide this for yourself, as there are many fanciers who use creosote.

PLANNING

It is cheaper, in the long run, to think out exactly what is required. The initial outlay may be heavier, but the time it will last and give satisfaction will be well worth while. A lot of money can be wasted in altering, adding and repairing unsatisfactory hutches. Give this plenty of thought and care.

Three tiers of hutches are usually best. However, four tiers of the smaller cavy type may be used for 'running on'. Don't stand hutches directly on the ground. Have them raised up, high enough for a cat to get under to stop mice from making their homes there.

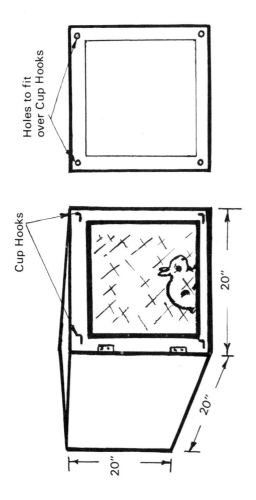

Holes to fit
over Cup Hooks

Cup Hooks

20"

20"

20"

Frame covered with Roofing Felt to fit
on Cup Hooks, to keep out draughts

SATISFACTION

A well constructed rabbitry will give more pleasure and convenience. It will save so much more time in attending to stock. It is worth while taking that extra bit of trouble at the start.

It will also save expense in the long run.

Single Tier Hutch

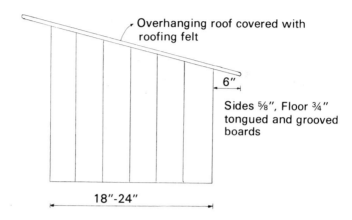

Overhanging roof covered with roofing felt

6"

Sides ⅝", Floor ¾" tongued and grooved boards

18"-24"

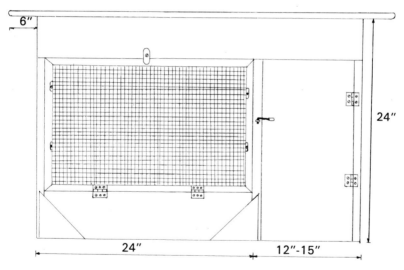

6"

24"

24"

12"-15"

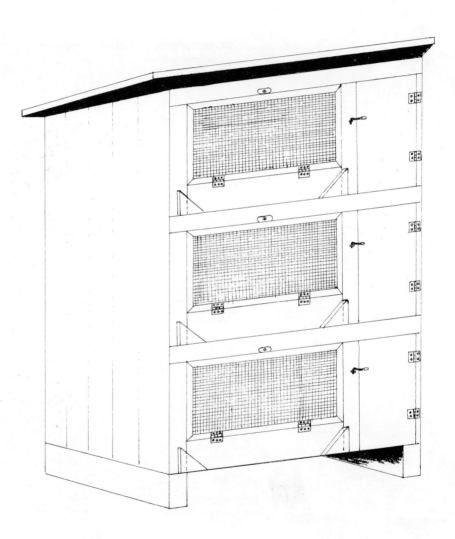

Three Tier Hutch

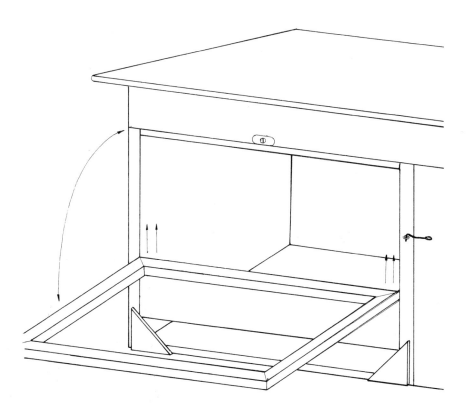

The meshed section of the door opens downwards on the hinges in order to allow feeding, but stopping any babies from falling out. To enable removal of soiled bedding the whole door section lifts out in the direction of the double arrows

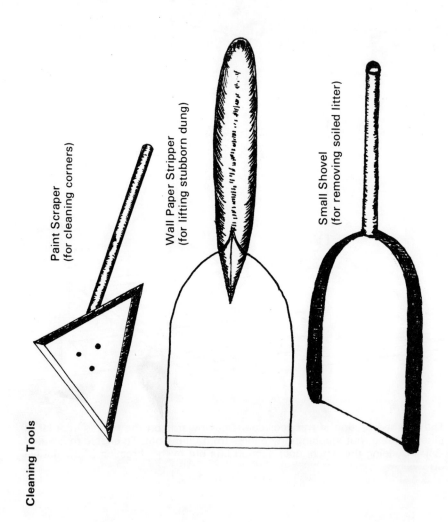

Cleaning Tools

Paint Scraper
(for cleaning corners)

Wall Paper Stripper
(for lifting stubborn dung)

Small Shovel
(for removing soiled litter)

CHAPTER 3

Feeding Methods

There is a very good reason for considering feeding as a first step. It is no good rushing out and getting stock of any breed, until you are completely ready to house it, have considered the many methods of feeding, what stock is available and what will best suit your pocket. It will pay dividends in the end, to put in some hard thinking and take all these decisions **before** bringing any stock home; otherwise you could end up by killing, albeit unwittingly, some very good or expensive foundation stock.

EARLY DIET

It is vital, at first, to follow the diet used by the breeder from whom you have purchased the animals. If your chosen method differs, changes must be made very slowly.

Begin by giving smaller quantities of the feed to which it is accustomed, adding very small amounts of the diet to be followed. About every ten days, substitute a little more of the new diet while reducing an equivalent amount of the original.Follow this ten-days-to-a-fortnight routine, and if all is going well, continue substituting more new diet and reducing the old and undesired diet.

If, for instance, you intend to feed pellets, but have acquired an oats and greenfood fed rabbit, withhold a little oats and add, roughly, half a dozen pellets. Always give water to pellet fed rabbits. Reduce the greenfood and encourage the rabbit to take the water. Eventually, you will safely have introduced the changeover of diet.

If at any time during this process, the rabbit appears in distress, or not coping with the changes, go back to the last change that was successful and follow it a little longer.

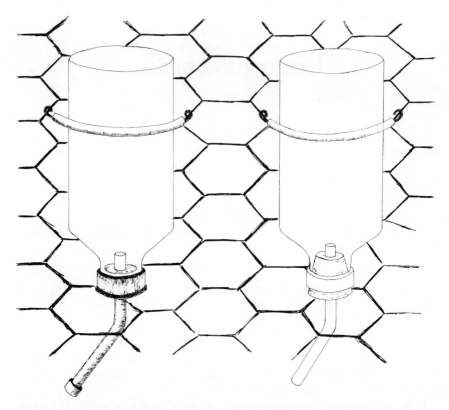

Manufactured bottle, with plastic screw-on top, aluminium tube and stainless-steel nipple.

Home made bottle with cork or rubber bung, glass tube with end softened in a flame.

Water

Rabbits need water. Although you may choose to feed greens, it is still advisable to provide water. Water pots may be used, but can easily be overturned by the rabbits. Excellent drinking bottles are now obtainable. They are advertised regularly in all the livestock papers and books. Medicine or small lemonade bottles, scrupulously washed out, are cheap, as only the rubber bung and glass or plastic or metal tubing need to be bought. Hang the bottle up in the hutch, preferably using a Terry clip round the neck of the bottle and secured to the side of the hutch and a piece of spring wire, with an eye clip pushed into either end to secure the upper part to two hooks screwed into the hutch wall.

If preferred, the nozzle may be pushed through the outer wire front and spring wire with a hook in either end will secure it to the outside of the front welded mesh. This has the advantage of being quicker to fill, as the hutch doors do not have to be opened, but in winter, water can freeze and the bottles will tend to crack, if it is an outside rabbitry. Aluminium tubes are best and most used today.

Teaching How To Use Bottles

If the rabbits are not used to this method they will have to be taught. They will certainly be curious and go to look at the bottles. Watch carefully to see if they learn what to do. If, after a short while, they have not found out how to obtain the water, they will require teaching.

Put their mouths to the bottle, moisten a finger and let them suck the finger. Then put them to the bottle again. Persevere and they will eventually get the idea.

A bottle can be useful, sometimes, for the giving of medicine, which can be put into as much water as they normally drink in a day.

Feeding Pots

The heavy earthenware pots, with turned in edges are to be preferred for food, as it is difficult for them to scratch out and waste the food put in. These can be purchased, or troughs made that hang on the walls. Be careful to get the height right.

CHEAPEST FORM OF FEEDING

Traditional oats and greens are possibly the cheapest form of feeding. A Dwarf will require good quality oats, crushed or whole; about

2 ounces per day for an adult. A handful of mixed greenfood will be necessary. Try to obtain a good mixture. A suitable list of these is included elsewhere in this book. For collection from the hedgerows, invest in a good wildflower book, with illustrations, coloured if possible for identification, as many plants are poisonous to rabbits.

WASHING GREENFOOD

If collecting from a market or greengrocer, wash thoroughly, as sprays may have been used. Wash anything from hedgerows, as it may have been fouled by dogs or other animals.

If a small patch of garden can be spared, many useful things can be specially grown, as, for example, chicory, kale (if a large rabbitry), cultivated blackberry (the fruit for home consumption and the leaves for feeding in season and drying for later). Cow parsley, strawberry leaves, raspberry and blackberry leaves are an excellent astringent, and can be dried for winter use. A piece of hard bread or toast is much appreciated. A **small** piece of some root vegetables is enjoyed and keeps the rabbit occupied, as well as being nourishing. It sharpens the teeth and keeps the mouth in order, promoting saliva.

The accent on all these things, with the Dwarf, is **small**. Only small quantities of anything should be fed, until you have discovered what suits each animal. Potato peelings, dried, are often relished, particularly by nursing mothers.

PELLET FEEDING

Pellet feeding is extremely useful. Time is saved, as greens do not have to be collected, sorted and washed. It simplifies feeding during the illness of a fancier as someone else can safely undertake this job without making mistakes, or making too great a demand on time. It is a balanced food, a very great consideration, especially for the beginner. A number of firms make special rabbit pellets and most advertise from time to time in *Fur & Feather*. There are slight differences in them. It is always cheaper to buy by the cwt and to collect if possible.

Get 28lbs (12.7 Kilos) at first, if you only have a small number of rabbits, until you find which brand suits your requirements. Buy this amount if you are intending to keep only a small stud, then they will not go stale. Adequate water must be given with pellet feeding.

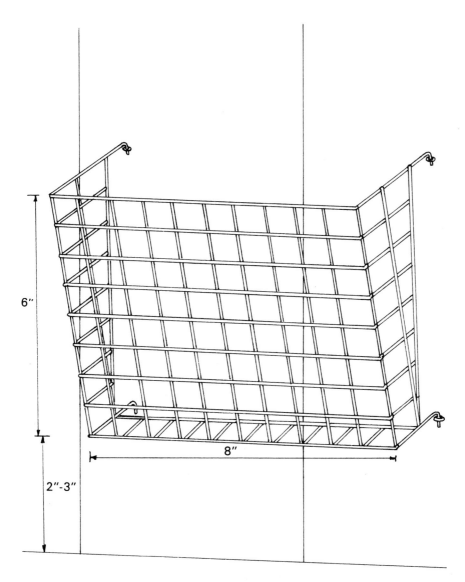

6"

2"-3"

8"

The hayrack is fixed to the side of the hutch by slotting into "eyes" which are screwed into the wood. The rack is 2"-3" above the floor of the hutch to enable rabbits of all ages to feed from it.

HAY

Whatever form of feeding chosen, give the best quality hay that you can afford, meadow hay if possible, as it contains that rich mixture so desirable.

FEEDING METHODS AND VARIATIONS

Feeding can be once or twice a day, dividing the day's total intake in half in the latter case. The diet will vary in quantity, quality, and variety according to the animal's occupation. Obviously a breeding doe with a litter requires more. She should have a container with plenty of food in it, in order to help herself, as desired.

The babies will start popping out of the nest from three weeks on, and begin to take an interest in the food. She needs plenty of water at all times. She may like a little root vegetable, while she is suckling young. Leave as much hay as she will eat.

Only feed adults as much as is regularly cleaned up. If food is left uneaten reduce the quantity until the correct amount is given.

MASH

Mash is not a suitable food for Dwarfs. It is messy, overheating and goes sour unless eaten up at once. The Dwarf has only a tiny stomach and cannot eat a day's requirement of mash at once.

RESTING DOES

A resting doe should not be overfed, as she will become overfat very quickly. Fat is also laid on around the ovaries, and she could eventually become sterile.

SHOW AND STUD BUCKS

A Show buck, going out regularly to shows, or a stud buck in regular use, needs to be well fed, but not allowed to gorge as much as he likes. With these, the aim is to keep them at the desired weight (around 2 lbs) and in hard condition. A hand over their haunches will soon tell if they are too thin. They should feel firm and hard, no bones. The eyes

Plate 1
Top: T. Stratford's Double Champion Red Eyed White.
Bottom: K. Ashford's Blue Eyed White.

should be bright and alert. They should come readily to the feed dish when it is filled.

BREEDING DOES

A breeding doe will not usually require any extra food for the first two weeks. Just increase the hay. Begin to increase the hard rations daily, then, to what she clears up.

This is an approximate day's estimate of required rations for differing uses. Other variations and needs will be found in later chapters.

J. Murray's Red Eyed White. *(Photographer, H. Bush)*

CHAPTER 4

Selection and Acquisition of Stock

The accommodation is now ready, and the choice of feeding method made, so stock can now be safely acquired. Visiting the shows, talking to breeders and travelling to studs, when possible, should have provided much useful information.

ADVANTAGES OF RED EYED WHITES

There are certain advantages in starting with the white variety. They have been established longer, there are more of them (if each colour is counted separately), therefore, there is a better chance of obtaining quality foundation stock. The added difficulties of blending colours in breeding plans is not present. All attention can be given to producing type and coat, while experience is being gained.

On the other hand, it is much harder to win or 'get in the cards' with a white, in an all white class, because of their present all-round excellence.

SELECTION OF FOUNDATION STOCK

Rules, however, for selection do not vary in general. The ideal beginning is a trio, comprising a good show buck and two related does. If this is not possible, a mated doe is the next best thing. The doe does not need to be a show specimen — indeed it is better if she is not; but she must be mated to the very best buck that can be afforded. It is important, also, that the buck is either the same strain, or has a large proportion of the same blood line in him. This can involve a lot of research which can be done while your preliminary arrangements are being made. First, then, the buck which is going to be the foundation of your Stud. The following attributes apply, therefore, whether it is a white or a coloured one.

FOUNDATION STUD BUCK

He must be healthy and strong. Look carefully at the nose. There must be no suspicion of wetness there, no sniffling or signs of a cold. The same goes for the eyes. If either shows any signs of having been 'runny'; any suggestion of wetness, he must be rejected at once. If there is any previous history of this trouble, it can usually be detected on close inspection. Look for any tiny tell-tale bare patches in the corner, or corners of the eyes, or suspicious shortage of fur. Do not be persuaded that it was only a cold. Once this trouble is in a stud, it is very difficult to eradicate.

This animal is the basis of all your future stock and is the most important purchase that you will probably ever make.

When satisfied about his health, what about his virility? He should look alive and alert and interested in everything that is going on around him. He should be well covered and in hard condition. The bones should not be felt on running a hand over the hind quarters. Inspect the genitals and all round that area very thoroughly. Is it clean? More important, is it all there? Feel the scrotum and make sure there are two testicles, fully descended. Remember, he CAN retract them, so don't hesitate to ask to revisit and see him again.

He must be small, weighing not more than 2 lbs. Short ears, not over 2 ins in length, well furred before and behind, nicely rounded at the tips. A big fault in Dwarfs' ears is a tendency for them to come to too much of a point, something which creeps in very easily. Be constantly on the look out for it. The ears should be carried erect, not lying back and not being crossed in any way, nor kinked, nor set too wide apart.

Ensure the body is well rounded and cobby, the rear feet tucked well under, the front feet short, neat and fine boned. The head should be well rounded, set firmly on the body, no neck visible, so that viewed from the back, it would appear to go straight into the shoulders.

Obviously this is perfection, so remember the essentials. Look for the best that can be afforded and is available. Faults can be balanced to some extent and weak points improved with the does.

FOUNDATION DOES

Purchase two does if possible. They must belong to the same strain as the buck. Somewhere in the pedigree, there must be some, as much as possible, of the same blood; i.e., relations. They must not be full blood sisters of the buck, not even if they are from different litters.

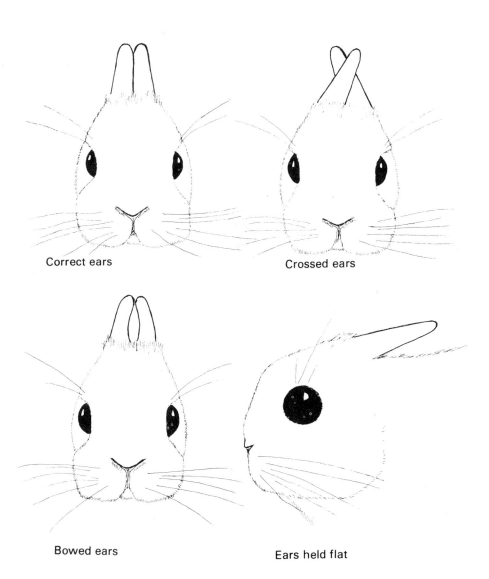

Correct ears

Crossed ears

Bowed ears

Ears held flat

One can be his mother, however, or his mother's litter sister. In fact, if her litter sister is available this would be an excellent start. The other doe should be related, but more distantly. Do not on any account start off with two sisters; this is much too close at this stage. If two such does are not to be found, get the best you can and ask for it to be mated to her sire or his closest relation, or the buck's sire.

As with the buck, thoroughly examine them for health. Pay particular attention to their vents, which should be clean and a healthy pink colour, unless in season, when they will appear swollen and purplish.

Next, examine the buck's weaknesses. Make sure neither doe shows the same one or ones. Always try for a good balance, being sure that any weakness in one is countered in the other. A little longer length of ear in the breeding doe is permissible (the accent is on 'little'), but never use a BUCK with poor ears.

The doe does not need to be a show specimen, but must be well bred from show stock. Does for breeding can be a little larger than show specimens, for reasons to be found later on in the chapter on Breeding. It does not matter if they are a little longer in body, provided this is not excessive.

If you are starting with whites, be sure the buck has a good eye, i.e. bold, rather like a pug dog, slightly bulging, as deep, glowing, ruby red as possible.

The coloured Dwarfs have eye colour to match their individual colours, but the shape and size should be the same.

It is highly unlikely that all three animals will come from the same stud; but it is possible the breeder can recommend another breeder, who has some of his stock or blood.

BREEDERS' REPUTATIONS

Don't be afraid to enquire about breeders' reputations. No honest breeder fears genuine enquiries; he will be proud of his reputation.

Importance of Seeing Relations of Foundation Stock

When buying the doe or does, ask to see some of the other relations, particularly the parents. Look at any litter brothers or sisters, animals sired by the same buck to other does. This is important, if she is not quite as good a specimen as was desired. Faults can be avoided by careful selection. Never countenance narrow skulls, snaky type, coarseness of any kind, white patches in coloureds (look in the armpits and under the chin and in the pads). There must be no doubling up of

Ears erect, rounded at tips, 2" or less in length

Round, bold, broad head

Round, bold, bright eyes

body short, compact, cobby and wide shouldered

Correct type of Netherland Dwarf

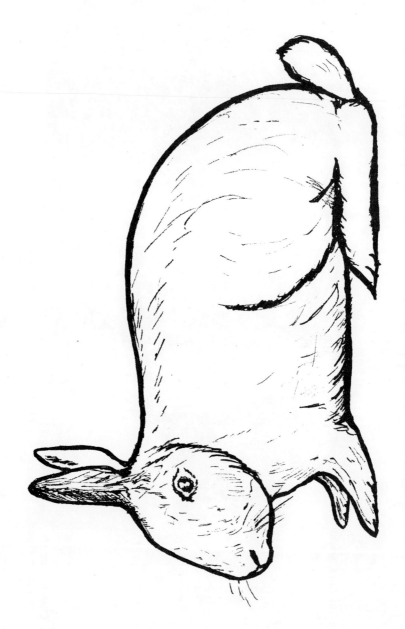

Reasonable breeding doe. (Ears slightly long, slightly longer in body than desirable for show. Should make a good breeder. Good shoulders).

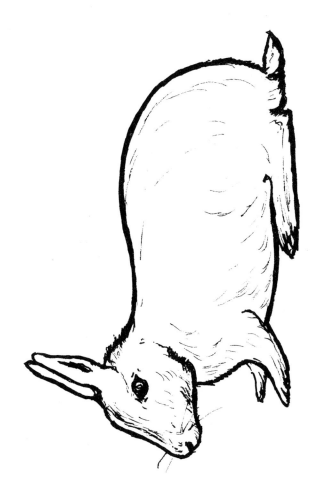

Poor type. (Ears too long, snipy face, long body without any depth, narrow shoulders).

any fault carried by the buck. A little longer or larger body, not quite such a good eye, or ears not more than 2½ ins can be allowed in initial breeding does, but nothing else.

In colours, watch out for white hairs in the ears or any white patches as opposed to the odd white hair in the body.

A doe for breeding should come from a proved sire of winners, or a winning buck, or have good show stock among her relatives. Hence the desirability of seeing her relations. I cannot impress this too deeply or too often. Use this as a guide line to get the best possible and improve and replace stock as better specimens are bred or become available.

ADDITIONS FOR COLOURED BREEDING STOCK

With coloureds, there are a few more problems in the initial stock. Some knowledge of what colours mix and what do not is necessary, whilst a novice. The blue eyed white follows the same rules as the red eyed white, except that it has a bright blue eye instead of red.

IMPORTANCE OF 'ROLL BACK' COAT

The Netherland Dwarf *standard* calls for a 'roll back' coat. This means a coat which, when a hand is run through it, from tail up to the nape of the neck, falls gently back into place, and does not fly back like a flipped pack of cards. This is required for all colours, including whites. Never be persuaded to use a buck or a doe that does not comply with this requirement.

ALTERNATIVE CHOICE

If a trio has not been available, the next line of choice will be a mated doe. For this, go to a reputable breeder.

In visits to Shows and studs a strain particularly liked may have been noted. Enquire if this stud is in a position to help. If not, someone may know who has some of the strain or stock with some of the blood. Get a doe from this source and either have it mated to one of the bucks, or perhaps the breeder you originally approached may mate it for you.

Do not be too fussy about the show standard of this doe. She should be roomy of body, healthy and strong, a little larger than one for show. The latter point is wise, certainly until some experience of

34

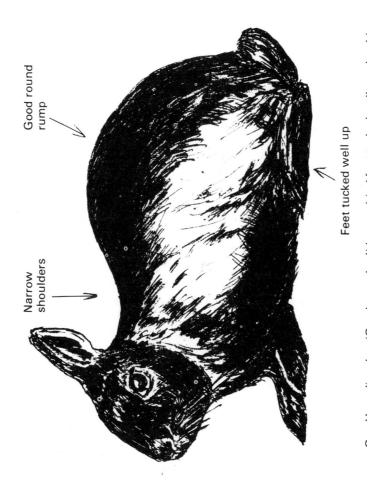

Good round rump

Narrow shoulders

Feet tucked well up

Good breeding doe. (Good sound solid rump, hind feet tucked well up, shoulders too narrow).

rearing litters has been gained. It will save disappointment possibly in early ventures. Do not be satisfied with one carrying serious faults, of course, but a well bred one from show stock with winners in her pedigree at fairly close quarters. Avoid like the plague the snipy head, the long body.

MATING THE FOUNDATION DOE

Great care must be taken with the mating of this doe. Take the advice of the breeder or owner. If this is the foundation of your stud, no one is going to blame you for being anxious and careful and wanting to see the sire and some close relations.

What to Expect

From this beginning, it is possible that a buck worthy to become the stud sire may be born. Something reasonably fit to show in local or small shows, however modest, should appear, however.

RINGING AND/OR TRANSFERRING

It is most important to ensure that all stock, when bought, is ringed. That is, wearing a British Rabbit Council ring on its hind leg (either one), which gives the year of birth and a number, which is registered in the breeder's name originally (and the present owner's, if it has changed hands). There is also a letter indicating the breed. Make sure this is an X, which is the letter assigned to the Netherland Dwarf. This number in its entirety must be transferred to your name, by sending it to the British Rabbit Council on the specially provided cards for that purpose, signed by the seller and yourself, with the required fee.

This procedure must be followed every time an animal changes hands. This registers you as the present owner of the rabbit and any progeny as yours as the breeder. You may not show a rabbit that is not registered in your name. Any progeny is the property of the owner of the doe and not the owner of the sire. Thus, it is important to attend to this matter as soon as possible after stock changes hands. It is also important to ring youngsters in good time, for this establishes your ownership and you as their breeder. If left too long, there may be difficulty in getting the rings on.

In early days, do not be persuaded to buy an animal that is not ringed. Breeders, obviously, are not going to ring every animal bred. This is a straight case of expense. No one will ring a buck that is obvi-

British Rabbit Council Identification Ring

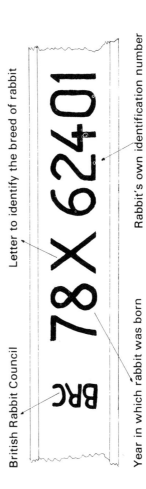

Letter to identify the breed of rabbit

Rabbit's own identification number

British Rabbit Council

Year in which rabbit was born

ously never going to see the inside of a show room. Most will ring a doe, however, even if she is not fit for show, if she is well bred from top quality stock, comes from a well sired litter and which contains a show specimen, PROVIDED she has none of the unforgivable faults. She must not carry any of the weaknesses carried by the stud bucks. She may well prove an excellent mother and have some useful babies.

RESULTS OF WRONG FOUNDATION STOCK

This method means waiting longer before you can make your debut in the Shows; but it will be a much safer and sounder way in the long term, than being tempted into buying a show buck, that is no relation to your does, for the sake of a few show cards, then finding out that he does not suit your does, and only rubbish is being turned out. Don't think this doesn't happen, because it can and does.

The best buck in the world will not necessarily produce anything any good, unless suitably mated. If he does, it could be a lucky fluke, that he suited that one particular doe. He may never do it again with that doe or any other. This is not the way to found a dynasty. Breeding within the strain is the only sure way to regular and consistent good results. Surely it is worth a little bit of patience.

Write up somewhere where you will constantly see it:

Never Buy Unrelated Animals To Found A Stud and Never Mate Together Two That Carry The Same Fault.

CHAPTER 5

Breeding

The best stock that can be afforded is now settled in the best rabbitry that can be afforded. A start can be made. Let us suppose that you have purchased a mated doe.

REQUIREMENTS

Nothing much different will be needed for a couple of weeks. Put her straight into the breeding hutch on arrival (or after mating, if you have your own buck). Larger hutches are needed for does with litters and it is best if she goes directly into one of these.

These should be fairly deep, from front to back, as well as long, so that the rear is out of the rain. One third should be divided off, by a solid partition, running two thirds of the depth of the hutch from the front to the back. This provides a dark and protected part for the nest and babies. It also leaves room for them to pop in and out of their day quarters and nest. Make sure that the outer door to the solid nursery quarters is separate from that of the front mesh part and has a really deep litter board.

BEHAVIOUR

The doe will probably make her nest right up against the litter board, as does usually choose the darkest corner. This has an advantage for you, when inspecting youngsters, but dangerous if there is no litter board, as they can easily spill out, when the outer door is opened.

Give plenty of hay and water, though she should not start nesting yet.

If mated to your own buck, put her to him again two or three days later. If she refuses him, she is probably safely in kindle. Do not let him pursue or pester her. If she is unwilling, remove her at once.

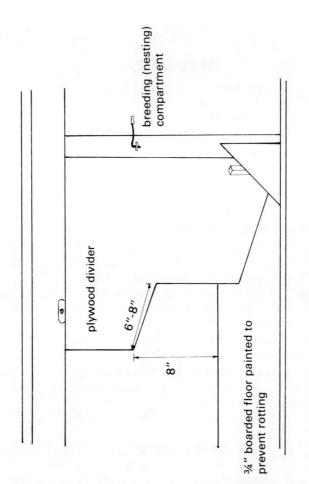

breeding (nesting) compartment

plywood divider

6"-8"

8"

¾" boarded floor painted to prevent rotting

Division between Breeding and Feeding Compartments

How To Mate — Behaviour Patterns Of Buck and Doe

To mate a doe, take her to the buck's hutch, NEVER the other way round. If a buck is placed in a doe's hutch, she will probably attack him.

To effect a mating, having put the doe in with the buck, stay with them and observe. The buck will stamp around with his back feet, making a lot of noise in the process and going after her. They may play around at first with the doe running away. If nothing happens, make sure the doe is in season; i.e., the vent is swollen and purple in colour, then return her to his hutch.

Matters can be assisted in the following way. Gently place the thumb on one underside of the legs behind the belly. Place the fingers on the other underside of the legs behind the belly. Gently raise the hind quarters up a little, taking care not to dig in, as this might injure her. The buck should then mount her from the back. If all seems to be going well, take your hand away and leave them. He will probably grab a piece of her fur on her back or neck, to steady himself and keep his balance.

If a successful mating takes place, he will fall off and may possibly utter a scream. Do not be alarmed, this is a good sign and quite normal. If he is prepared to mount her again, let him; but don't let him exhaust the doe, if she is unwilling. You will only be frustrating him and laying the foundations for a bad tempered buck, as well as tiring the doe.

Sometimes, with a vigorous young buck, he does not want to let her go and can become very nasty at interference. The only thing to do is, either to remove him to a travelling box, or discreetly distract his attention with some choice titbit of greens that he likes, while you remove the doe.

Should she begin to run about after two weeks from mating, carrying hay in her mouth, it is probable that she is not in kindle. Return her to the buck and remate. The litter should arrive approximaltey thirty-one days after mating. A day or two either way gives no cause for concern.

Successful Mating Behaviour

About two and a half to three weeks after mating, she will begin deciding where to make her nest, carrying hay about, pushing sawdust up into little heaps until making a final decision. She may try several places first. Then work begins in earnest. A few does are lazy and do the whole job just before kindling.

She will push up sawdust, pat it down, and may turn round and wet it. She is making a good solid base. When she is satisfied with this,

Lifting to assist Mating

BREEDING

(a) Buck mounts.
    Holds doe by back

(b) Doe rises, extends
    hind-quarters
    and buck penetrates
    doe and falls sideways

(c) Buck dismounts
    or falls off

(a)

(b)

(c)

Stages in mating

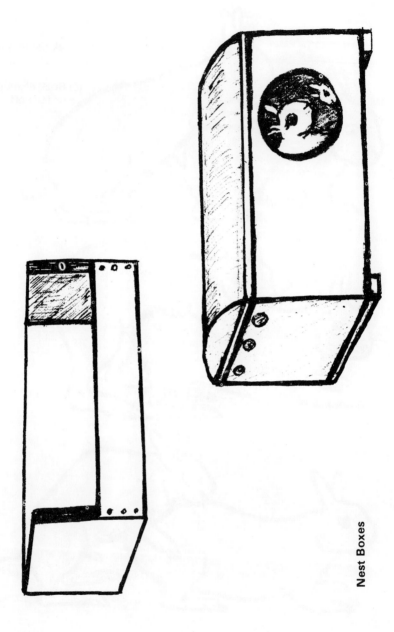

Nest Boxes

bits of hay will be deposited on top. She will create a good depth, and, considering what a small amount can be carried at once, this is very hard work for her. So make sure that there is always plenty of water to drink.

Towards the end of her time, she will pluck the fur from her chest to make a soft lining. She may even strip her belly bare and be quite nude underneath. Do not disturb her at this time, talk to her when feeding and make a little fuss of her, if she appears to like it. Otherwise, leave her alone.

NESTING CHOICE

Hope that the inner compartment will be chosen. This is most likely, as she will want darkness and privacy; but if she starts building in the outer compartment in earnest, in the early days, it can be moved inside sometimes. Put some hay inside and hope she will take the hint. If she persists in ignoring the suggestion you will have to leave things alone. Just make sure that she has extra protection from the weather.

FEEDING THE PREGNANT DOE

After two weeks, increase the rations, a little at a time, giving just as much as she clears up. Continue adding like this until she is due. Keep plenty of good quality hay in the hutch, she will eat it as well as her rations, if necessary.

Know Your Does' Habits

The fur pulling is rather variable. Some does only do it immediately before kindling, some begin several days earlier. The ones that leave it to the last minute can be worrying to the new fancier, especially if the doe is new to him also. Once a doe's habits are known, it is a different matter.

Problems Encountered in Rearing Litters

A Dwarf usually has about two or three in a litter. If she is a small show specimen, she may only have one and this brings problems.

The first serious problem in this case is warmth. Warmth is more important than food at first. Two or more little bodies can cuddle together and keep warm. A Dwarf baby is **very** small. All baby rabbits chill easily and a Dwarf can die of cold **in the nest** even in fifteen min-

45

utes. So be somewhere around at kindling time, if possible. Be very unobtrusive, as a mother will kill her babies if she is under the impression that there is any kind of danger.

What is Danger in a Doe's Mind?

Danger, in her mind, would be loud, sudden, or unusual noises, a stranger in the rabbitry, even you, coming too close. It is essential, with Dwarfs, to ensure that the young are put safely in the nest and covered up, when they are born. It is a delicate situation; that is why it is best if does are used to being handled frequently and know their owner really well. That is one reason why I always made a habit of beginning to talk quietly — to myself, if necessary — some little distance before arriving at the rabbitry. I try never to take them by surprise.

How Young Are Born

The doe usually knows what to do and will do it. Each baby is born, normally quite easily, in a sac. The mother tears open this sac and out pops the baby, all wet and sticky. She washes it and eats the afterbirth and sac. This is where trouble sometimes occurs in a young maiden doe. While she is eating the afterbirth, she may, while licking the baby, accidentally tear a leg or some part. Tasting the blood, she thinks it has to be cleared up and eaten. Thus, she may get labelled a cannibal, quite wrongly. So a poor little mangled corpse is found. Don't discard her, remate at once. Only discard her as useless if the performance is repeated.

Each one will, normally, be put in the nest before the arrival of the next. Nature seems to arrange these matters very well. She will pull more fur off, when kindling is finished and cover the nest. She will need a long drink of water and will suckle her babies at once before taking any rest.

Nest Boxes

Some breeders use nest boxes. Very good ones can be bought or made. Many breeders do not. The big disadvantage as regards Dwarfs is that if a baby gets pulled out of the nest accidentally, for example, if the doe is startled while feeding and jumps away — a baby hangs on to the teat and is pulled out. It is blind, so cannot find its way back over the barrier. It remains outside the nest and soon dies of cold. If found in time, it can be put back.

If it is very cold and lifeless, put it down inside your shirt for a few hours, where your body warmth may often revive it. Or put it in a cardboard box, lined with hay. Place this on top of a radiator, or in the airing cupboard on top of the hot water tank. This can be done with sick, or deserted babies.

Proximity of Bucks

Keep stud bucks away from breeding quarters, especially. They should always have their own quarters, if at all possible, in any case. Some of them will be going off and returning from shows frequently, causing disturbance, often late at night, if returning from some distance and by road. They are also being groomed regularly every day and prepared or trained for show, so there is usually a lot of activity where they are.

This causes quite a lot of noise and does not give the breeding does the quiet and peace that they need. Stud bucks can be a real nuisance, as they are noisy, constantly stamping and smelling strongly. The doe will resent this and their presence very much.

Dogs are a particular danger and can be very frightening to a new mother.

Advantage of No Nest Box

If the nest is left to her, she will probably use two or three sides of the hutch for her nest, and the fourth will be open, thus any baby can crawl back in and under the pile of hay and find its mates. This is the advantage of an inner compartment and no nest box.

However, have a good look round at the varying nest boxes available, each has its special features, then make a decision. There is no guarantee that the doe will use it, of course.

Suckling and Weaning

The doe will suckle her babies for three weeks approximately, then they will begin coming out of their nest. They will begin to take an interest in the food dish and the water bottle. These may have to be lowered for a few weeks, so that they can reach them. Be sure there is an extra supply of food on hand when the young start to eat. The doe will eat less herself as she gradually ceases to suckle them. At six weeks old, the young should be completely weaned.

SPECIAL PRECAUTIONS

Be watchful when there are litters about. See that there is always plenty of bedding of soft, warm hay in the hutches at night. If outdoors, cover with sacks or draught boards to keep out fog, rain and/or damp.

Watch for any sudden drop in temperature and give extra bedding. A coming weather change can often be foreseen. The mother doe is a splendid weather prophet. If she is to be seen stripping off more fur and piling it on the nest, for no apparent reason, then be quite sure she has sensed the coming cold, and is making provision for it. Give her more hay and an extra sack. When the weather is about to be unusually hot, she may well open the top of the nest by day, and carefully cover it up again at night.

DANGER FROM COLD

The danger period is from now to four months. A youngster that has crawled out and been unable to find its bed, may die of cold; but if a hutch full of good hay is there, it may burrow down and survive until found the next morning, by you or its mother. This applies to youngsters recently separated as well as to those still with their mothers.

SEPARATION

Take the doe away at six to eight weeks. Leave the babies in the breeding hutch and remove the mother, never the other way round. If there are only two babies, it may be wiser to leave the doe for eight weeks, but if three or more, take her away at six weeks.

They can usually grow on together, without fighting or trouble, until between ten and twelve weeks old, when they will require separating into individual hutches. Cavy hutches are big enough for one youngster to have plenty of room to run around, but small enough to be cosy.

FEEDING OF WEANED AND SEPARATED YOUNG

Do not overfeed. About one ounce of pellets, gradually stepping up to one and a half, plus plenty of good hay, should be adequate until five months. You can add a piece of hard bread, if you wish, as well. The rabbit will enjoy this and it will keep it occupied and interested for a considerable time.

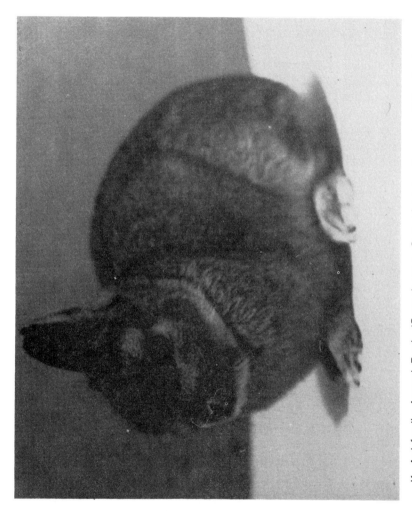

K. Ashford's Agouti Buck. (Superb type. Son of triple champion 'Wooding's Wonder'.)

OBSERVATION

Observation is the best teacher of each individual baby's needs. Handle regularly, and if in good hard plump condition, but not fat, then all is well. Bony haunches and spines can soon be felt, if sufficient is not being fed.

If you have chosen to feed pellets, a decision will have to be made as to whether to feed those containing an anticoccidiosis mixture (an anticoccidiostat), or plain ones.

In some areas, only plain ones are available. (You can, of course, obtain a mixture to add yourself, but there is no certainty that the rabbits have actually taken the required amount.) In some areas, only those containing the coccidiostat are available, and in other areas, it is possible to get both.

So, if you wish to use them, make fairly extensive enquiries in your neighbourhood among ALL the chandlers and animal foodstuff warehouses. It is usually a matter of which particular brands are stocked. There are likely to be several brands available in cities or large areas, whereas smaller places may only be able to afford to keep one brand and you will have no choice, unless you go further afield.

You can tell the brands that contain the anticoccidiostat, because the bags are stamped with the letters ACS (anticoccidiostat supplemented).

'Embazin'

'Embazin' is the trade name of a popular mix and much used by manufacturers; there are others and, at the time of writing, there is another mix undergoing trials. As yet, it is not available on the open market.

Changes

Changes are constantly being made to these added mixes, indeed new pellets come on the market from time to time, so it would not be of any real help for me to recommend or mention any particular brands.

Where to Find Information — Anticoccidiosis

Most makers advertise extensively in *Fur & Feather*, trade magazines, and animal books and publications. However, you will always find those containing an anticoccidiostat clearly marked on the bags. They are good and worthwhile, as coccidiosis is a terrible disease. It strikes at all ages and spreads like wildfire through a stud.

It is a danger that Show stock must run. They can so easily pick it up at a Show from a 'carrier' and bring it back with them. This alone makes it a wise choice to use the pellets and do your best to keep your own stock immune. If they come into contact, there is some protection and may prevent them from being affected.

CLEANING OUT DURING SUCKLING PERIOD

Clean out the outer breeding compartment as required; but leave the nest part alone. Scrupulous cleanliness is the keyword. Use a good disinfectant powder on the floor under the sawdust. Use an aerosol for flies in and around the rabbitry. Sweep up daily after feeding or cleaning is completed.

The doe will scatter the nest when it is no longer required and the inner compartment, or where she has chosen to make the nest, can then be cleaned out.

COCCIDIOSIS

Coccidiosis is the most feared disease and spreads most quickly among adolescents. No one is 100% sure of how it spreads, it may be by flies or mosquitoes. The germs are certainly on the floors of hutches, so mice running about can carry it. Prevention is the only real hope.

INFECTED HUTCHES

If there is any suspicion that an animal has died of it, clean out the hutch, burn all litter, scrub out with ammonia, which is the only known disinfectant that really touches this disease, and leave it to dry. When it is dry, use a blow lamp on it, particularly in the corners, repaint and leave the hutch unused in the fresh air — sunlight if possible — for as long as you can.

Isolate all stock that has been in contact or in nearby hutches.

INFECTED STOCK

Do not attempt a cure with sick adolescents with this disease. **Kill them**. It sounds brutal, but it is the wisest course in the long term. Once an animal is infected, it should never be used for breeding. It could be a carrier, so it is not fair to other exhibitors to show it.

51

MATING PROGRAMMES

There are a lot of things to consider in a mating programme. The primary thing to remember is never mate two animals together with the same fault. (Check your records, also, to see if one is **carrying** this fault, although hidden from the eye.) This is doubling up the trouble and making it even more difficult to eradicate.

CHOICE OF BUCK

Never use a buck with ears over 2 inches in length and/or weighing over 2 lbs.

DISADVANTAGES OF SHOW DOES

A show doe is not always a satisfactory mother, as she is very small. A Dwarf does not usually have any difficulty in kindling, but it is wise to try to avoid small mothers. A show doe may not take kindly to motherhood, not be suitably placid, after the excitement of a show career, plus the more important fact that smaller does will probably have smaller litters, giving less selection, or indeed producing only one baby giving rearing problems. In fact, only one in the litter can often be a disaster. If it is not warm weather, it is very difficult to keep enough warmth in the little body and it may die.

Naturally with only one baby suckling, nature usually arranges that not so much milk will be produced, but it will still get far too well fed and grow too large; which is bitterly disappointing, should it be a good one.

CHOOSING A NON-SHOW DOE

Use a slightly larger than show doe, one that is beautifully bred from show stock, either sired by a winning buck or having show specimens in her brothers and sisters, or from a buck that has produced winners close to her.

She MUST be related to the buck and if she is his daughter, excellent. She will be carrying fifty per cent of him, so mating her to him (still bearing in mind the essential *no doubling up of faults*) should increase the buck's qualities, at any rate in some of the resulting young. She is likely to have a more placid temperament and a larger litter, thus giving a better chance of a decent one, with none getting too much milk.

Son to Mother

A son to mother mating is another good choice. Remember, however, that faults can be more easily doubled in this case. Bear in mind, that what is actually seen in a rabbit is only what was dominant in the breeding. It is not the whole story.

Recessives

There are things called *recessives*, which do not show up, if an animal dominant in that respective quality mates with it. If, however, both are carrying this particular hidden (recessive) quality, then it may well show up. This is why complete and accurate records of all animals must be kept.

Doubling Up and Correction Of Faults

All these preliminaries apply equally to white or coloured Dwarfs. With the coloured Dwarf, the problem of colour complicates things. Some colours are dominant to others. Having the ideal pair type wise is not enough. Both may have white armpits, or pads, or frosty noses, or putty noses, or white toenails. The list is endless.

Consider **type** problems first; this will leave you with a short list of possible matings. Now study the other faults of these, one at a time, and make a short list. You will eventually be left with just a few possibilities. Choose the pair, or pairs, with the characteristics most needed to correct faults or improve or imprint on the Stud.

Sables and Smoke Pearls

Smoke Pearls and Sables with little or poor saddles might be the problem. Find one excelling in this. Never forget the cardinal rules for bucks, **not over 2 lbs and ears not over 2 ins in length.** Perhaps a Marten Sable has not as much ticking as is desired. Look for one excelling in this for mating to it.

Do not breed light sables to light sables all the time, they may start to get rather 'mealy' in colour. Some breeders do this, but they are all very experienced people, who know what they are doing. Use a good **dark** to a very **light** or a nice **medium** to restore the colour. If a Marten doe has a frosty nose and you MUST use her because of either other good points, or you have no choice, then find a dark Siamese Sable buck for her and be careful not to mate the progeny too close for a while, the exact opposite of normal practice.

53

If Smoke Pearls become pale and lacking in shading, introduce a Sable occasionally to restore colour and saddle. Don't do it too often. There are successful breeders, who regularly mate Smoke Pearls together, but, again, they are experienced. Nowadays it is possible to do this; but these are breeders using all the years of hard work that have gone into breeding true Smokes.

RULES AND RECORDS

Serve an apprenticeship first. Learn to work to rules before attempting to break them. An artist breeds colours and mixes and matches, *after* he has mastered the first steps. Most important of all in colours, **keep records**.

A rabbit that regularly throws a serious fault, however mated, **get rid of it,** no matter how good it is in other respects. Once strongly implanted some faults are terribly difficult to eradicate.

Blacks

Have a Black buck excelling in colour; a solid, glossy black going right down as far as possible. Remember that the buck will put the largest percentage into the stud. The colour is very important in Blacks. The under colour is slate blue. Breed always from black, blue, or occasionally Agouti stock.

Avoid Blacks that have come from Sables. A few decent ones may turn up, but in the long run the correct under colour will be lost, the Black will become dull, muddy, or rusty. Blues can safely be used, if they have no Sable in them. They must be true Blues!

Blues

Breed Blues with Blues and the occasional Black or Agouti (the Agouti is used for its good type and eye). Avoid the Sable bred Blues, they are not the right shade at all, usually poor Smokes with no saddle, and very likely having the wrong undercolour. Remember it must be a clear Blue and not a dirty or greyish shade.

Banded and Mixed Colours

Take care to distinguish between the three banded and the two mixed colours, like Agouti and Steel. Use a Black occasionally if you are beginning to lose depth of colour in the Steel.

The Opal and the Lynx are extremely beautiful, and an occasional true Blue may be used.

Chinchillas, at the time of writing, are breeding true, though they sometimes turn up in Agouti litters, as do Squirrels and other colours.

In mixed litters, great care is essential in recording ALL antecedents.

Tortoiseshell (these have been around for a long time, under different names, the Madagascar and the Sooty Fawn being two of them). They are most attractive and can be used to produce some charming other colours, such as Fawns, Beiges and Oranges.

Agouti

The Agouti is one of the most useful (unless breeding Whites, of course, or Sables).

Every stud should keep a top quality Agouti buck and doe. This is the original wild colour, from which all rabbits first came. Any colour can be produced by selective mating from it. The Agouti has a long show life, and is one of the best for type and especially eye quality. Thus, with great care and careful records, this colour can be most useful in a coloured stud.

Blue Eyed Whites and Colour Bred Red Eyed Whites

Two other points must be borne in mind. The blue-eyed White is not a true White, that is to say, not an albino. Neither are red-eyed Whites which crop up in coloured litters. Experienced judges can usually tell whites that have come from coloured litters. Do not breed with them with colours. You will, eventually, get white hairs creeping in.

HINTS ON BREEDING COLOUREDS

Visit as many shows as you can to get the best idea of the colour you are aiming at. Study the full size breed variety. Remember to be concerned only with the colour, not the type. A Dwarf must conform to the Dwarf *standard* first and foremost. Go to a well known Dwarf breeder of the colour desired and ask him to point out why he likes a particular rabbit's colour. Ask why he does NOT like that of another. Ask him to point out its faults and how he might be thinking of improving it.

Don't be afraid to ask a judge's opinion after a show. Tell him you are a beginner first, then ask him to explain what he liked about the winner and where some of the others failed. Most judges and breeders are only too pleased to help and advise.

There is a large scale model for every colour Dwarf, study them as often as possible, paying close attention to the exact shade, shadings and markings. Nothing else, just colour. After you have done this, a good basic knowledge will have been gained and some idea of personal likes and dislikes formed.

WISEST CHOICE FOR BEGINNERS

Don't aim too high at first. Choose just one or two, preferably colours that go together. In contrast to Whites, more than one colour will probably be required to have the necessary ingredients for correcting faults, or maintaining a proper balance. Therefore, in your early days, stick to related colours and do not be too ambitious. Choose Blacks and Blues, or Sables and Smokes. Then, perhaps, when these principles have been mastered others can be added as desired.

Start with the more conventional and established ones. There is one exception, that is, keep a good Agouti. It is the backbone of the colours and can be kept with almost anything except Whites. It can provide almost any colour, suitably mated, and because of its all-round excellence, typewise, it is a useful and worthwhile member of any coloured stud.

Plate 2

Top: Mrs. Rita Musk's Dark Marten Sable (11 months old. Note good markings and saddle).
Bottom: K. Hazell's Marten Smoke Pearl (note good mask and saddle).

Plate 3
Top: D. Pepper's Champion Blue. (First Champion to be registered in this colour).
Bottom: E. Addison's North Eastern Young Stock Show winner, Dark Siamese Sable Doe.

CHAPTER 6

Colours

PITFALLS

Inevitably, some matters discussed here are already partly covered in other chapters. What are some of the pitfalls to be expected? There are several common to all colours. White hairs in ears or white patches on the body colour are obvious; but another, very difficult to eradicate, are white patches in the armpits and on pads. These last two are frequently found in Blacks and Sables.

SABLES

Sables have problems with their shadings and saddles. This applies both to the Siamese and Marten variety. It has been fairly fully dealt with in the chapter on Breeding.

TICKING

How does the novice distinguish between 'ticking' and white hairs? The standard says, 'any ticking extending up and over the flanks is an added beauty'. Ticking is found on Marten Smokes and Sables, Fox Dwarfs and other Tan patterns. It is a sprinkling of white tipped hairs over the flanks, rump and body.

The operative word is 'tipped'. If the white goes the full length of the shaft, it is a white hair. If the shaft is coloured with only the tip white, then that is 'ticking'. Experience will soon teach which is which. This may seem elementary to some readers, but it is surprising how many it puzzles in their early days.

'FROSTY' OR 'PUTTY' NOSES

Another problem for these colours is 'clean nose and ears'. Only by very selective breeding can this be achieved. Never on any account use two 'frosty' or 'putty' nosed rabbits together, however great the temptation.

A 'frosty' nose is a sprinkling of white hairs around the mouth and nose, whereas a 'putty' nose is a white patch in the same place, or it can take the form of a small white streak just above the lip, running up into the nose. It is sometimes very faint, the rabbit can then be shown; but never use it for breeding. This may sound hard, but mistakes made at the foundation stage of a Stud can take bitter years to undo; indeed, some never.

If you **must** use one with a little 'frost', then be careful to get a Siamese Sable for a mate, as dark a one as possible. Start on the right lines and save future heartbreak!

THE USEFUL AND BEAUTIFUL AGOUTI

The Agouti is a most useful colour as well as beautiful in its own right. The colour is one of the best developed, type-wise, of all the coloureds, and usually excels on broad skulls, with prominent, bold eyes. It should have a bright overall chestnut shade, with plenty of black ticking all over.

It has much in common with the wild rabbit, but should be brighter, richer and sharper. The desired chestnut shade still tends to be rather brown as a rule. The bright orange band in between is still not as bright as wanted, tending to be more 'muddy'; but vast improvements are being made, as this is written, and there are some really good specimens to be found. The undercolour is slate blue and this is now very well established.

In Agoutis, look out for these 'muddy' shades, 'definition' that is not clear, sharp and distinctive are not wanted. Nor is 'banding' that is jagged, or chinchillation of the feet. The Agouti is susceptible to white pads and armpits.

DEFINITION

What is meant by 'definition'? It is *the sharp distinction between the bands of colour*. They must not run one into the other, but be clear and definite (hence the term 'definition').

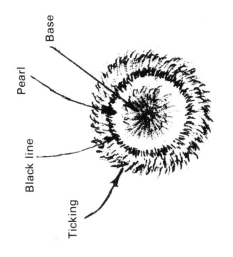

Base

Pearl

Black line

Ticking

Parting the fur
by blowing

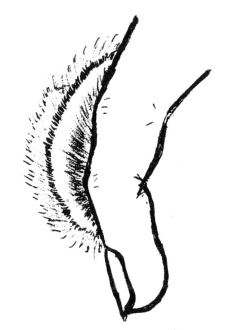

Definition

Parting the fur
with finger to show
definition of Agouti pattern

The Agouti patterned Dwarfs all have white bellies with appropriate undercolours, white eye circles and white undertails.

MOULT

An Agouti in moult is always muddy and patchy. This is quite normal. Moult also takes the form of blurring the 'definition', because the different hairs are all moulting at different times. Time cures this, as the moult clears; but do not expect time to do this if it was never clear in the first place. Obviously, *avoid* purchasing an Agouti pattern when it is in moult.

Moult is a perfectly normal event. Every rabbit has its own pattern of doing it. It is simply changing its old coat for its new one, like a dog does.

CHINCHILLAS AND SQUIRRELS

It would seem appropriate to include the Chinchilla and Squirrel here. They follow the same pattern but are different in colour.

The Chinchilla has a black outer band over a middle band of pearl, and a slate undercolour, with black guard hairs, giving a sparkling blend of black and white mixture. If you blow into the fur, you will see the Agouti banding, only in the different colours.

The Squirrel is a sparkling mixture of *blue and white*, having a blue band over a pearl middle band and a lighter slate undercolour.

Any doubt should, therefore, be cleared up by the overall colour, black or blue. The undercolour cannot be a *certain* guide, because a Squirrel with a too dark undercolour and a Chinchilla with a too light undercolour can be confusing. Only experience can teach these finer points, but the overall difference of black or blue should be easy enough for anyone.

Look for clean lines between the bands, unless in moult, no colours smudging or encroaching on others.

Brownish Tinge On Chinchillas

Occasionally, there is a faint browny or fawny shade on the backs of young Chinchillas and Squirrels, which comes from their Agouti ancestry. Do not discard these, the brown may well moult out as the full adult coat comes through. If it does, this is often the best rabbit in the litter.

Many Chinchillas (and Squirrels) are *too pale*. Imagine a normal size Chinchilla rabbit and put a Dwarf type (i.e., ears, body and head) on it. This should give you an accurate picture of what colour is wanted.

OPAL

The Opal is one of the most beautiful of colours, resembling that lovely semi-precious stone. The fawn and blue combining to give a shimmering rather than sparkling effect.

It can be distinguished from the others by its middle band, which is fawn. It has a slate undercolour, but the blue on top is lighter than that of the Squirrel. In the Opal, there must be no 'ticking'.

If breeding this colour and getting too sandy or muddy a look, introduce a good blue. This must be done with great care, for it must be a true blue of excellent colour, and true bred. Do not do this more than once in about five generations.

LILAC

The Lilac is an extremely difficult colour. People disagree as to what is meant by 'pinky dove grey'. Any tendency to blue, however, is wrong. The colour should go right down to the skin. It is a self colour.

BROWN

The desired Brown is a dark chocolate colour, and, again, it is the undercolour that will be the problem. There are many very dark Siamese Sables about, that the novice could easily mistake for Browns. Here are two pointers. A Sable, however dark, **must** have some shading and some saddle. Scrutinise it very closely and you will find it, however slight. The Brown is a self colour and has no shading.

The other pointer is our old friend, the undercolour. In the Sable, the body colour must go right down as far as possible. The Brown has a definite undercolour; it is pearly grey, completely different.

TORTOISESHELL

Of the other varieties, the Tortoiseshell is probably the most frequently seen. This, again, is a most attractive colour and is still often

61

referred to as the Sooty Fawn. The overall effect is as if soot had descended on it, and the rabbit has given itself a good shake, leaving a light dusting. The Tortoiseshell should have an orangy saddle, shading down on the haunches to blue/black. The belly colour will be lighter, of course, and it has a bluey white undercolour. The ears and mask should be an attractive mixture of blue/black.

ORANGE

The first Orange was bred by the author and this became a Club Champion. It came from experimenting with Tortoiseshells, Opals, and Agoutis. The main problem with this method is getting rid of the light sooty dusting.

FAWN

The Fawn is similar to the Orange, except that the one should have a bright orange saddle and the other a warm fawn one. Both shade off slightly down the flanks to a white belly.

BLACK AND BLUE

Both these colours have been dealt with extensively in the chapter on Breeding.

HIMALAYAN

The Himalayan is well established and breeding true. It comes in four colours. The ears should be coloured to the roots. The front feet should be coloured as far up as possible and the hind feet as far as the hocks. These are called the 'stockings'. The nose has an oval patch of colour as far up as possible and right down into the whisker bed. The tail is coloured. The body is completely white. It is very attractive indeed.

STEEL

The Steel is a two-colour mixture, black and steel, giving an all-over pattern of steel. It must never be confused with the Agouti pat-

Himalayan "Stockings"

terns. The undercolour should be a very dark slate and there must be no hint of any kind of 'banding', like the Agouti patterns.

The steel colour is maintained all over, mask, feet, tail, ears, etc.

If the colour begins to look a little dull or indistinct, a really good type, deep, true bred Black, can be introduced, but not more than once in five generations. Avoid using an Agouti, if possible, as problems with browny tinge and banding will begin to crop up later.

UNSTANDARDISED COLOURS

These are colours in the making, so it is impossible to say what they are. They will be constantly changing, as each one becomes true breeding and is granted a standard. See separate chapter.

SEAL POINT

The Seal Point, long a favourite with the Americans, was not recognised in Great Britain until some time later.

It is something like the Himalayan in that it has a dark mask, feet, tail, ears, etc. The body colour is not white, but shades off from the rich sepia of the extremities to a lighter shade. This must be quite distinct and it should in no way resemble the saddles of the Sables.

THE NETHERLAND DWARF STANDARD (as at 1978 - 1980)

TYPE (FOR ALL COLOURS)

BODY. Short, compact, cobby, and wide shouldered.
Devoid of raciness. Front legs short, straight, fine in bone. 30 points
EARS. Erect (not necessarily touching), well furred,
slightly rounded at tips. Desired length 50 mm (2ins)   15 points
HEAD Round, broad skull.   15 points
EYES Round, bold, bright.   5 points
COLOUR. Only those colours listed separately shall be
admissible, except in classes staged solely for
unstandardised colours at Netherland Dwarf shows.   15 points
COAT Soft, short, dense, roll back.   10 points
CONDITION   <u>10</u> points
    <u><u>100</u></u> points

WEIGHT Desired weight 0.9 Kg (2 lbs)
FAULTS Narrow shoulders; ears not erect, bent or overlength; narrow face. White hairs in coloured rabbits and black hairs in blues; fly back coat.
DISQUALIFICATIONS Racy type, crooked legs; odd coloured, wall, or speck eyes; white patches; white armpits; putty noses. Exhibits weighing 0.9 Kg (2 lbs) or over in u/5 month or u/14 week classes, exhibits weighing 1.13 Kg (2½ lbs) or over in Adult or Any Age classes, but if the exhibit in the opinion of the judge is overdeveloped for the age of the class it should be disqualified irrespective of weight. Overgrown or mutilated teeth. Running eye(s).

Group One: Selfs

WHITE As pure a white as possible, creamy or yellow tinge a fault. Eye colour ruby red **or** rich dark blue.
BLACK A rich lustrous black, slate blue undercolour, brown tinge a fault.
BLUE A clear, bright, medium shade of blue (not lavender) throughout, from tip of fur to skin.
BROWN A rich dark chocolate, colour going well down the fur with a pearly grey undercolour.
LILAC A pinky dovegrey throughout, from tip of fur to skin. Bluish tinge a fault.

Group Two: Shaded

Sable (Siamese) Medium

To be a very rich sepia on ears, face, back, outside of legs and upper side of tail, the saddle colour shading off to a considerably paler colour on flanks and belly, the dark face colour to shade off from eyes to jowl to blend with the chest and flanks: all blending to be gradual, avoiding any blotches or streaks, and consisting of a soft and varied diffusion of sepia shadings. The dark colour on back to extend from head to tail. The chest to be of the same colour as flanks and the whole fur to be absolutely free from white hairs. The undercolour to match the surface colour as closely as possible, following the varied shadings throughout.

Sable (Siamese) Light

As medium, but colour to be 'rich sepia'.

Sable (Siamese) Dark

As medium, but colour to be 'very rich, dark sepia.' N.B. The main difference in the three colours is the width of saddle, in *tone* and *intensity* of Sepia colour.

Smoke Pearl (Siamese)

The saddle to extend from nape to tail to be smoke in colour, shading to pearl grey beige on flanks, chest, belly, and to be totally free from white throughout. Head, ears, feet and upper side of tail to match saddle as near as possible. All shadings to be gradual, avoiding blotches or streaks, general undercolour to match surface colour as closely as possible following the varied shadings throughout.

Seal Point

A rich, dark, sepia brown on ears, nose, feet and tail. Shading to a lighter colour on body. Eye colour to be dark brown. **Faults**: Blotchy colour on the body; body colour too light or too dark so as to lose the decided contrast between the body colour and the marking colour.

Group Three: Agouti Patterned

Agouti

A rich chestnut shade, with black ticking over an intermediate orange band and a dark slate blue undercolour. Ears laced black. Eye circles, underside to tail and belly to be white with slate undercolour.

Opal

Top colour pale shade of blue with a fawn band between this and a slate blue undercolour. Ears laced blue. The eye circles, underside of tail and belly to be white with slate undercolour.

Lynx

Orange-shot-silver. Intermediate colour to be bright orange, clearly defined on white undercolour. Tips of fur silver. Belly, eye circles, inside ears and underside of jowl white. **Serious faults**: Bluish tinge on top, blue undercolour.

Chinchilla

To resemble real Chinchilla. The undercolour to be dark slate blue at base, intermediate portion pearl. (Slate to be definitely wider than pearl), with black narrow line edging; pearling to be clearly defined: top grey, brightly ticked with black hairs, either even or wavy ticking admissible, neck fur lighter in colour than body but strictly confined to nape: flanks and chest ticked with uniform shade of pearl slightly lighter than body: eye circles light grey-pearl, well defined: ears laced with black.

Squirrel

A sparkling blend of blue and white, with blue ticking over an intermediate pearly-white band with a light slate undercolour. Ears laced blue, eye circles, underside of tail and belly to be white with light slate undercolour.

Group Four: Tan Patterned

Tans

Body colour to be either black, blue, chocolate or lilac, and to go down the fur as far as possible, with undercolour of appropriate self colour, belly, chest, eye circles, inside of ears, underside of jowl and tail and triangle to be rich tan. Face and outside ears to match body colour.

Foxes

Body colour to be either black, blue, chocolate, or lilac and to go down the fur as far as possible with undercolour of appropriate self colour. Chest, flanks and feet to be well ticked with white guard hairs. Eye circles, inside of ears, underside of jowl and tail, belly and triangle to be white.

Sable Marten Medium

To be very rich sepia on back, ears, face and outside legs, and upper side of tail, the saddle colour shading off to a paler colour on flanks, the dark face colour to blend with chest and flanks, all blending to be gradual, avoiding any blotches or streaks and consisting of a soft and varied diffusion of sepia shadings, the dark colour on back to extend from nape of neck to tail: the chest, flanks, rump and feet to be well ticked with longer white hairs, any extension of ticking over sides and rump to be considered an added beauty and not a fault, but ears and saddle to be free of white hairs, the light nape of neck to be confined to a triangle behind the ears and to be as small as possible; eye circles, inside of ears, line of jaws and belly and underside of tail to be white. General undercolour to match surface colour as far as possible, and the varied shadings throughout.

Sable Marten Light

As **Medium** but colour to be rich sepia.

Sable Marten Dark

As **Medium** but colour to be very rich dark sepia.

Smoke Pearl Marten

Saddle to extend from nape to tail, to be smoke in colour, shading to pearl grey beige on flanks and chest. Head, ears, and upper side of tail to match saddle as near as possible. Chest, flanks, rump and feet to be well ticked with longer white hairs, the light nape of the neck to be confined to the triangle behind the ears and as small as possible. Eye circles, inside the ears, line of jaws, inside nostrils, inside legs and feet, belly and underside of tail, and triangle to be white. The colour under white belly fur should be fawn.

Group Five: Other Varieties

Orange

Bright orange saddle shading down the flanks. Colour to go well down the fur with a white undercolour. Chest to match flanks. Eye circles, inside of ears, underside of jowl and tail and belly to be white.

Tortoiseshell

(Formerly Madagascar or Sooty Fawn). Rich orange saddle gradually shading to a blue black on the flanks, haunches and belly. 'Points' bluish black. Top colour to go well down the fur with a bluish white undercolour.

Steel

To be bright steel throughout. Head, feet, ears and belly to match body colour. Colour to be as free as possible from a brown tinge. Undercolour dark slate, carried down to the skin, with no trace of grey or yellow band. Underside of tail may be a paler shade than body. **Faults**: Feet and ears not matching body colour. Barred feet.

Himalyan (The Himalayan Dwarf is recognised in all four colours). *Black* 'Points' to be black. Body colour pure white. Nose markings to go well up between eyes, into whisker bed, to be large and egg shaped. Ears dense colour to roots. Front feet markings well up legs and down to toes, tail dense to roots.

Chocolate. 'Points' to be rich, dark chocolate.

Blue. 'Points' to be light medium blue.

Lilac. 'Points' to be a rich even shade of dove grey.

Fawn

Warm fawn saddle, shading down the flanks, colour to go well down the fur with a white undercolour. Chest to match flanks. Eye circles, inside of ears, underside of jowl, tail and belly to be white.

CHAPTER 7

Exhibiting and Preparation for Show

There are many technical aspects associated with showing stock. One does not buy good stock of exhibition quality, or breed likely specimens and just take them along, hoping for results. Much work is involved. The following deals only with the Netherland Dwarf. If later, other breeds are added, it cannot be assumed that their show preparation will be the same.

Presentation

Whites must be spotlessly clean. Dirt will accumulate on an exhibit during the day, particularly if it is doing well, as it will be getting a lot of handling in the Duplicate classes. A good judge, who saw it at the beginning of the show in its straight class, will know if it started out in a proper condition, and *may* make some allowance for this. Later on, in the final stages, when it comes to **Best in Show**, condition is bound to go against it, if its opponent is an equally good specimen of another breed.

Another hazard is if there is more than one judge, the other one has not had the opportunity of seeing your rabbit at its best, earlier on. He can only judge on what he is actually looking at.

Washing

One possibility is to wash a white rabbit prior to the show. This is a perfectly good idea provided certain precautions are taken:
1. Be careful to make sure it is dry and has cooled off before returning it to its hutch.
2. Use an absorbent towel or cloth first, then finish off with a small hand drier.

The main snag with washing is that it softens the coat and affects the natural resistance and resilience. So, if a preliminary wash is to be given, give it several days beforehand to give the coat a chance of recovering its normal feel.

Hutch Cleanliness

Scrupulously clean hutches are of the utmost importance for the prevention and control of disease as well as for the keeping of stock in show condition. Keep a good depth of sawdust under hay topping, so that urine is well soaked up.

Types Of Sawdust

Be careful what sawdust is used. Enquire what wood it is, before using it for Whites. There are some woods which, when wet, turn red. Mahogany is one of these. It is not so important for dark colours, but disastrous for the more delicate shades.

Washing Of Feet Only

An alternative to bathing, and preferable in my opinion, is the use of an old, soft toothbrush. The night before a show, settle down with the exhibit, or exhibits, and their newly cleaned out travelling boxes. Have ready a tooth brush, a saucerful of warm water, a jug of hot water to use for changing when it becomes dirty and some mild soap. Always change the water in between each exhibit as well. The soap must be white.

Wrap the rabbit in a soft towel or piece of cloth and get to work on the paws. Wet the brush thoroughly, well soap it and brush away gently, but firmly, first at the tops of the feet and then a little harder at the pads and between the toes. The accent is always on gently. When they look reasonably clean, change the water (this is very important at this stage), carefully dab each paw in the saucer, one at a time. Dry thoroughly with the soft towel.

The feet will be a little damp after this. It is impossible to get them perfectly dry, nor is it even desirable. Put it in its box, *not* a hutch, and make sure the box is securely fastened. It will immediately start to give the paws a good clean and should make an excellent job of it. Done just again before they set off on a long trip, this ensures arrival with clean feet, as well as giving them something with which to occupy themselves on a long journey.

Cleaning The White Coat

Now for the coat. A chalk block, such as used for dogs, is by far the best for this. This does not do away with the natural 'feel' of the fur. Rub well into the coat all over. With a soft baby brush, brush it well

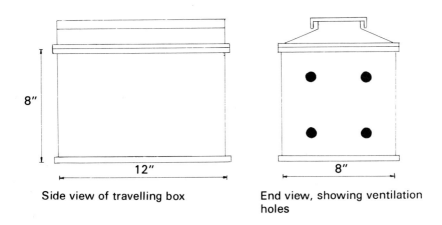

8"

12"

8"

Side view of travelling box

End view, showing ventilation holes

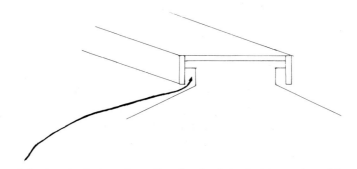

The top of the box is designed to allow fresh air in, but keep draughts out

out. This should be done a few days before the show and again the day before. One thing is vital to remember. Every vestige of powder must be removed, not a single scrap left in. If the judge runs his hands up the coat, as he will, and so much as one puff of powder rises up, the exhibit will be disqualified. The investigation Committee of the British Rabbit Council will investigate it as a case of undue and unfair preparation.

It is not using the cleaning agent that is wrong, it is leaving some in the coat, which obviously makes the rabbit *look* whiter than it really is, which is the trouble.

Unfair Preparation

The distinction between what is unfair preparation and what is perfectly permissible is a very fine one. Fanciers have been arguing about it for years and will continue to do so for many more.

The best guide line to follow is what the British Rabbit Council states on the subject. It simply states that the rabbit must be shown in its *natural state*. This would surely mean that there is no interference with what it had at birth. In short, *patches* of hair that are the wrong colour may not be pulled out or dyed. Wrongly placed lines or ragged lines may not be 'tidied up'. No cleaning agent may be left in the coat, that would give the impression that it is a better colour than it is. No colouring matter may be used to disguise a fault in a marked rabbit.

There is a duty to a breed to show it at its best. This means being **healthy, in good condition and clean**. Clean it to the best of your ability and knowledge, therefore, so long as all cleaning agents are completely removed. After all, it was born clean.

Cleaning Coloured Varieties

Follow a slightly different programme with coloureds. A chalk block is obviously not necessary. It may not always be essential to clean the feet. If you must, then omit the first wash and only do it just before the animal travels. It should only be necessary if rabbits are very badly stained for some reason.

Spend the time on brushing the coat each day, until it gleams. By far the best method is the old custom of spitting on the palms of your hands, then grooming hard. Continue to spit, if and when the hands become dry. This will remove all the dead hairs which make the coat look lifeless. It also gives a nice shine.

The final gloss is the final touch. This is achieved with a piece of pure silk material. Nylon will not do, it must be pure silk. Smooth the rabbit down daily, while it is showing. Polish it till it gleams. Then it

Plan view of single
Compartment travelling
box

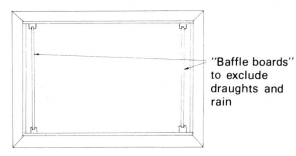

"Baffle boards"
to exclude
draughts and
rain

Plan view of three compartment travelling box

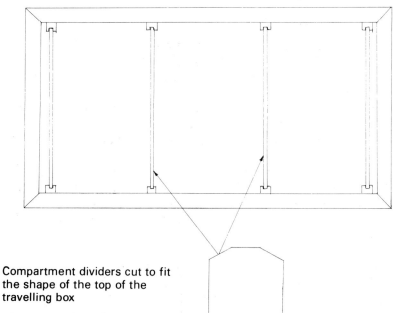

Compartment dividers cut to fit
the shape of the top of the
travelling box

will stand out among the others and catch the judge's eye straight away.

Toe-nails

Keep the toe-nails cut. It is very uncomfortable for the rabbit if its nails are overgrown. It cannot sit properly or stand so it certainly cannot show itself to the best advantage. Also, the dew claws (that is, those small ones growing part way up the inside of the front legs) will begin to dig into the flesh, as they curve round. Long claws on the feet will curl round and under.

At best, they will prevent the rabbit from sitting properly and at worst they, too, will cause pain and disfigurement. Some judges will not accept this condition on the show table, on the grounds that the exhibit is not in show condition. It is a very easy thing to attend to and, therefore, is inexcusable.

Preparation Of Travelling Boxes

Always see that rabbits travel in clean boxes, with plenty of bedding. A good supply of hay is useful, as if there is any delay on the return journey, it will be eaten, and could save a rabbit's life, perhaps, in an emergency.

Anything unfamiliar can upset a rabbit's stomach; alternatively, it may refuse to eat the strange food. Therefore, be careful what is put in the box for travelling rations. If pellets are fed at home, it is a good idea if the animals are familiar with oats as well. Plenty can be put in the box and will not soil the exhibit. They are a safe food as well as clean; ideal for long journeys. They are frequently fed at shows. The animal will scratch around in the travelling box looking for them, and will not get stained. They provide some interest on a long journey and prevent boredom.

Water is an essential with pellets, but this cannot be put in the box. If stock is used to root vegetables a small piece of something juicy can be included, but be careful it is nothing that will stain.

Get good travelling boxes. The rabbits are going to spend a lot of time in them. They need to be comfortable. It is false economy to scrimp on these, as they will have to stand up to a considerable amount of wear and tear over the years. Take note at shows — better still help with penning stock and getting rail stock away. It will soon be seen the kind of treatment they must be able to withstand. There are plenty of advertisements in *Fur & Feather* and trade magazines of various kinds you can purchase.

Early training table
(note sacking securely fixed)

Making Your Own Travelling Boxes

You may be the kind of person who can make your own boxes. So much the better as you can take the things you like from various types, and incorporate them as you wish, as in the case of hutches. They will need to be as light in weight as is consistent with the work required of them.

The important thing is to get the size right. What is the use of saving a little money and ruining your chances of winning?

A Dwarf needs room to move about, to turn round, plus height to stand up on its hind legs. Do not go to the other extreme, however, and have them too big. The animal may get thrown around inside, even, perhaps, injured. Go for the right amount of room combined with maximum strength allied to adequate lightness.

'Baffle' Boards

Do make sure there are 'baffle boards' which permit air without draughts. These are small boards at each end of the box, slotted down inside the outer sides. The outer sides have air holes bored in them and draughts will blow through into the box. The rabbit will be unable to get out of them and could catch cold or pneumonia, and will probably develop 'runny eye'. In any case, it is cruel to leave it to travel in such discomfort and misery.

ENTRIES AND CHECKING

Make sure to read the final date for the receipt of entries correctly and to send yours off in good time.

When the labels arrive, check them to be sure all exhibits have been correctly entered in all classes desired. Check train times, if they are going by rail and allow plenty of time for boxes to arrive. If going by road, allow time for holdups, diversions, bad road conditions, fog, or any other contingencies.

It is wise to enter ring numbers on boxes and labels, even if this has not been specifically asked. Should wrong penning occur, as sometimes happens, or exhibits be returned to a wrong pen during judging by a careless steward, this can often establish quickly the correct pen number and classes for which the exhibit has been entered.

Make sure you understand the meaning of the classes in the schedule. A common mistake for beginners to make is to enter their exhibit in the Breeders class, under the impression that it is the rabbit that is a proved breeder. This is not so. It is the **exhibitor** that is the breeder i.e., he or she has bred the animal in question.

Teaching a rabbit to "sit cobby"

STRAIGHT BREED CLASSES

It is compulsory to enter in the straight breed class first, before anything else can be considered. This is the class catering for a specific breed. *(See* Chapter 12.)

After you have done this, you are free to choose from among what are called the **'duplicates'**. Some shows mark these with an asterisk or the letter **D**: but don't bank on it. Which of these you enter will depend on your pocket and whether you may have a reasonably good exhibit, that might expect to do well in competition with other breeds. *(See* Chapter 12.)

If it is a promising one, you may like to try it against some from other sections; but it is wise to get someone to help you with your first attempts at filling in entry forms.

USEFUL TIP.

Do not overlook the fact that others are also governed by their pockets. Not everyone will be entering every class for which their rabbits are eligible. So quite a modest exhibit stands a chance of some nice cards sometimes, simply because rabbits that beat it in earlier classes have not been entered in them all.

HOW AND WHAT TO STUDY AT SHOWS

Take every chance of looking at winners at shows. Try to see why one was placed above another. Study the Dwarf *standard* till you know it off by heart.

As progress is made, you will find that you do not always agree with the placings. That need not bother you at this stage. In the beginning try, if possible, to study the placings of Dwarf Panel judges rather than the 'all rounder'. Get it firmly fixed in your mind what a Dwarf should look like. Study your own minutely.

This exercise will serve two purposes.

1. When deciding next year's mating plans, you will already have knowledge of what you lack and what you possess.

2. You will be able to see what good points you have with which to catch the judge's eye.

WHAT IS A 'SHOWMAN'?

Now you must set about teaching your Dwarf to be a showman. It must learn to show off its best attributes and to improve its weak ones. As previously said, a well shown exhibit can sometimes beat a

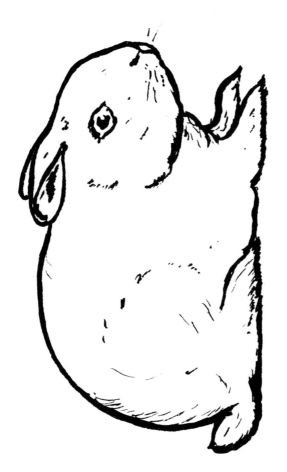

Ears lying flat — spoiling an otherwise good Dwarf

basically better one, that just won't perform, so the judge is unable to assess it properly.

TRAINING FOR SHOW

A show specimen is of little use, unless it is also aware of how to perform. After a stud has become well established and has been line bred or 'in bred' for a number of years, certain characteristics will be imprinted on the stock. By good and regular training in the foundation days, a certain amount of natural showmanship can reasonably be expected. Some will show better than others, some not so well; possibly even in the nest days they can be picked out very quickly. Often a reasonably typed specimen can always be trained to look a good deal better than it is basically. What is the use of the finest rabbit in the world, if the judge simply cannot see its best points, because it is bent on hiding them? This does happen.

Earliest Training

Begin training as soon as practicable. There is no hard and fast rule. Concentrate first on getting them used to being picked up, held, put down and handled in general. Some will take longer than others. Wait, of course, until the mother is happy to allow this. Cuddle them, make them feel there is nothing to be frightened about. You will soon find which babies are most amenable. In time, most will enjoy this and gain confidence.

Never force a youngster further and faster than it is ready to go. This means patience, as all have their own in-built inhibitions. These have to be overcome with care. Once it is happy with you, you are ready to proceed.

Second Stage

You will have got a table or bench or some place, where you are accustomed to putting down your feeding dishes and cleaning apparatus. This is where the next step takes place.

As soon as the baby is ready to be put down without hurling itself to the ground, put it down on this table. First cover the table with a clean piece of sacking to give the youngster some kind of grip. If it slides about and cannot keep its feet, you are going to end up with a very frightened and unco-operative pupil.

Let it run about, always keeping your hands near, in case of danger. Once it is quite at home, either in your hands or on the table, it

80

must learn to sit quietly there. This is entirely unnatural to it. Put it gently down and leave your hand lightly on the back, restraining it gently. It probably will not like it. Just keep bringing it back. Very slowly it will get the idea and learn to stay.

This is where its chances can be made or marred, where it should begin to become a showman.

PRODUCING THE 'COBBY' TYPE

Think all the time of the *standard* and what it *should look like*; cobby of body, no neck, the head going straight back into the shoulders. This can be achieved if a start is made in time. Do not allow bad habits to develop when young.

Place your hands lightly behind the ears, thumbs on one side and the fingers on the other. Make a stroking movement. Stroke as you would a cat, only, as you proceed towards the rump, press a little harder and make the pressure a little firmer, at the same time pushing the rear end up towards the head. This will also push the rear hind legs up under the body. They should lie quite straight there.

The idea is to prevent 'sitting long'. A well rounded short coupled body is wanted, the exact opposite of some breeds that call for a snaky long body. It may take quite kindly to this and soon get used to it. Keep at it. There is only one way to the top — hard work, regular and consistent.

Consistency

Once serious training has started, never let it slip with any exhibit. Even if it is not a training session, never let it 'sit long'.

This practice helps another desirable characteristic. The *standard* calls for ears erect. They do not have to be touching all the way up, but they definitely look better if they are, and this can be encouraged, as the pushing up of the body begins behind the ears.

Holding Ears Erect

While the rabbit is on the table, place the palm of the hand upright, fingers behind the ears, holding them straight up. Keep them there for several seconds, then take them away and repeat the action. Do this several times. Gradually it will learn what is expected.

Importance of Patience

Never lose your temper and never shout, it will become frightened

81

and confused. Always make a bit of fuss, when it has done well. Rabbits love attention and affection.

Training Table

Look out at jumble sales for any little, very small round table — a wine table is suitable. Alternatively, use a small box on top of the table in the rabbitry. When the rabbit is big enough and quiet enough to sit on your hand, sit it on this. The box should be small enough that it only just fits on. In this way, the rabbit will naturally 'cob' up the body in order not to fall off. As soon as this can be done, let all further training take place in this rostrum.

One other thing, when still tiny, teach it to sit still in the palm of your hand.

Vicious Exhibits

If a rabbit is really vicious, a decision will have to be made whether or not to keep it. It is not always a straightforward or easy decision. It may be an exceptionally good show specimen. It is not unusual to find that, though it is a demon at home, it behaves well on the show bench. On the other hand, it may be impossible to steward and to handle.

One thing is absolutely definite, it must never be used for breeding. You must make your own decision about its value, purely on its show potential.

Final
Training
Table

83

Good travelling box (open and closed positions).

CHAPTER 8

Ringing Your Exhibit

RING ESSENTIAL

No rabbit can be shown, other than in **Pets or Condition Only** classes, without an exhibition ring on its hind leg. How and when does one attend to this? It is important, as the procedure varies with different breeds.

Dealing purely with the Dwarf, if done too early, the ring will be constantly slipping off. If left too late, it will not go on. Only time and constant practice will give the 'feel' for this.

Always inspect newly ringed youngsters daily, to ensure the rings are still in place. Discover if any are missing before it is too late to rectify the loss. If any are not in place search the floor of the hutch. This can be time consuming, because of the tiny size of the ring; but it will be there somewhere.

HOW TO PUT IT ON

It is important to bear in mind the following fact. The Dwarf is a miniature animal, its bones are delicate, not like those of a Chinchilla Giganta, for instance, and it is very easy to break one. The bones of all young rabbits of this age are mainly gristle; but even gristle can be irrevocably torn.

A good idea is to get an experienced breeder to do the ringing for the first few times, and then to have early attempts supervised.

First Method

There are two methods. Either hold the baby rabbit upside down in the crook of the left arm (presuming you are right handed), hold it firmly, whilst with the other hand stretch the leg to its full extent, so that the forepart, the hind part and the hock (or joint) are in a straight line.

The rabbit may object or struggle. Release it at once and start again. Always be aware of this delicacy of bone structure and the ease with which it can snap.

Once the rabbit is reasonably still, slip the ring over the first obstacle, which is the thicker fur found on the paws and around the toenails. This is not bone, apart from one small bit, so be fairly firm about this part of the proceeding. The ring should now slip quickly up to the most serious obstacle, the hock, or elbow joint. This is where the biggest danger will be encountered.

The leg must be *fully* extended and in a completely straight line. With luck, the ring will slip over easily. A good deal of the bulk encountered here is fur, not always bone; allowance must be made for this in deciding whether to press on.

Never, ever, continue to hold a Dwarf by force, for ringing purposes. Release it at once at any sign of struggling and start again.

Second Method

The other method is one usually used on larger breeds, but can be useful with difficult Dwarfs. Tuck the animal's head firmly under the left arm, again straighten out the hind leg, as already described, getting it in an absolutely straight line, then follow the same procedure.

If the animal is extremely unco-operative it may be necessary to wrap the animal in a piece of sacking, leaving one leg out. Skill and judgement will come with practice.

There is one way of straightening the leg, which sometimes helps.

When the baby is upside down in the left arm, extend the leg by placing your left thumb on the leg joint (what would be called in a human, the knee). Press down firmly on this and the leg will automatically extend itself. Hold your thumb there, while you try to slip the ring up and over, with your other hand.

With a little practice, it often works. If you have any difficulties at all with any of these methods, wet the hock (joint) thoroughly, soap it well, push all the fur up in the wrong direction to which it is growing, i.e., the direction in which the *ring* is going, and soap the inside of the ring. Then push the ring up and, being slippery, it often slides very much more easily.

SOME USES OF RINGS

There are many practical uses for these rings, apart from showing. Records of a variety of matters are vital for the breeder. Which animals regularly transmit certain desirable, or undesirable, character-

Ringing

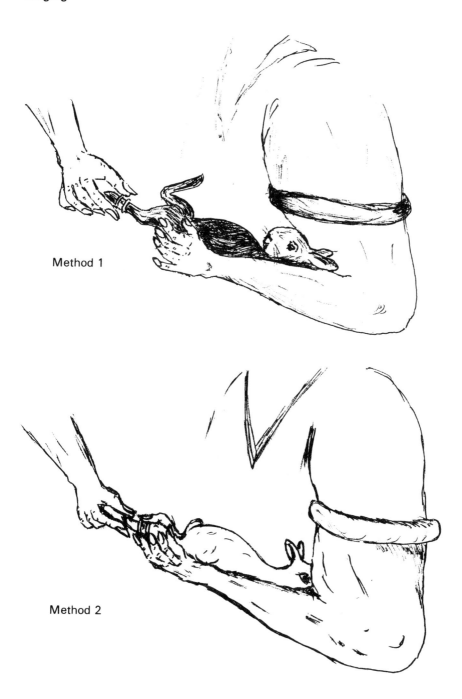

Method 1

Method 2

istics? Do they do this of themselves or only to particular bucks? Which does rear their litters well? Which are poor mothers, but, perhaps, produce good stock? Which animals produce only rubbish? Which bucks are good 'getters', always proving fertile, ready and willing? What are their records as regards quality of stock; are there a satisfactory number of show specimens to warrant their keep? Can certain bucks be relied on to deal firmly and adequately with difficult does?

All show results of every animal should be recorded, plus its abilities later as a getter of good stock.

Another use for the ring is to ensure that the rabbit which returns from a show is actually the rabbit sent. Always check this, mistakes *do* occur.

RECORDING

Evolve your own system of recording, according to what information is required, adding to it as time goes by. Keep individual records for each animal, plus a system of cross indexing on Subjects. The more you record, the better you will know your stock.

This can pay real dividends and save a lot of time, when next year's mating programmes are being planned, deciding which are unprofitable to keep, which are best destroyed, and which are not actually needed, but could be happily and confidently sold.

When a prospective customer comes along, find out what is wanted, and the records will quickly tell if there is something suitable and if it is for sale. Perhaps there is nothing actually for sale, but a knowledge of requirements and a knowledge of records, may be able to suggest a possible mating, or even where some suitable stock to the strain can be found at present.

Little things like these can quickly give a breeder a name for fair dealing and also helpfulness. People do not forget assistance willingly given.

Admittedly it is a chore at first, but get into the habit and it will soon become a pleasure. A really intimate and detailed knowledge of stock will be acquired quite subconsciously.

Incipient illness can be spotted in very early stages. By studying the records, problems that are not related to the stock at all, but are faults of management, can be traced. Furthermore trouble may be able to be avoided, even perhaps the unnecessary getting rid of an animal. This in itself is a worthwhile reason for the keeping of records.

Coloured Cards

Use different colour cards for different subjects, but preferably

Plate 4

Top: R. Chatfield's Chincilla Buck (Quintuple Champion)

Bottom: E. Addison's Chinchilla Baby (one month old, showing excellence of head, ears and body − requires careful training).

Plate 5
Top: K. Hazell's Himalayan
Bottom: Mr. and Mrs. L. Cumberpatch's Double Champion Agouti. (Note the beautiful colour but in full moult).

To put the ring on the rabbit, stretch a hind leg so that the hock joint is straight, rub the fur the wrong way, soaking the foot and hock with liquid soap, the ring will slide onto the leg easily. Clean off the liquid soap after ringing the rabbit.

use the same colour in each section. Some examples spring readily to mind, **red** for bucks, **blue** for does, **green** for the particular year.

Coding

Work out a colour code for such things as proved sires, proved sires of winners, sires dominant in certain qualities, sires producing regularly certain qualities (the two latter are not necessarily the same thing). An animal may possess an attribute but be unable to transmit it, whereas a litter brother or sister may not show it, but may regularly pass it on.

Does' show records, does' breeding records, complete with information on approximate numbers per litter, producers of winners or show specimens, good mothers, scatterers of litters (in this category, records of her other attributes will help decide if she is worth keeping and fostering her young at birth).

Cannibals

Never use a proved cannibal. Young mothers with first litters do sometimes eat or mutilate their babies. In kindling, the doe eats the afterbirth (placenta). In her eagerness, or if she is nervy, she may inadvertently eat part of a leg or head. Tasting blood, she may think she has to clear this up.

If it was an accident, she should be perfectly satisfactory in future. Give her the benefit of the doubt and do not label her a cannibal the first time. She may have been very thirsty. This may be *your* fault? Make a note on her records and watch subsequent behaviour.

Special Records

Record anything appearing regularly, in the matings of the same two animals; for example:

Deformed teeth. Viciousness.

System

It will become easy to plan a system after a little practice, and when decisions concerning specialisation have been made.

It will be seen, from these rough suggestions, that some animals will appear under a number of different headings. Therefore, at the end of the records, have a separate compartment containing the name and ring number of each animal, with the colours under which their information can be found — a quick way to find a good sire, a regular winner, a doe producing good stock etc. — with all other attributes that animal possesses as well.

Rings

These are purchased from the British Rabbit Council, B.R.C. Offices, Purefoy House, 7 Kirkgate, Newark, Nottinghamshire.

Make a rough estimate of needs for the year and buy a number at once. At certain periods of the year the B.R.C. is busy and there is a delay in getting further orders off. This can prove fatal in the case of the Netherland Dwarf.

IMPORTANCE OF RECORDING VISITING DOES

Make sure every mating of a visiting doe is recorded in detail; which the buck used, date of service or services, if remated, name and address of owner, date of does' arrival and despatch back to owner, and date of receipt of owner's letter to inform you of safe arrival.

Note any owner who does *not* so inform you. This can save a lot of trouble should any query from a dissatisfied owner arise, or a complaint be made to the B.R.C. at a later date. It is impossible to remember with any degree of accuracy all that has transpired over a period of time.

Cavy hutches (for "running on" Netherland Dwarf youngsters).

CHAPTER 9

Rabbit Clubs

The initials B.R.C. stand for the British Rabbit Council. If you wish to exhibit you must join this ruling body of the breeding and show world, similar to the Kennel Club for dogs and the Cat Council for cats. It makes the rules under which shows are held, safeguards the rights of fanciers and fights for them, when any trouble threatens.

The B.R.C. supplies the show rings, with which an exhibit must be ringed, before it can be entered in any show. It keeps a register of who is the present owner and who bred it and arranges the transfer, when any animal changes hands.

RULING BODY

The ruling body is called the National Council. This consists of members, democratically elected annually by postal ballot by every full member of the Association. Great Britain is divided up into areas and each area has a representative on the National Council. Some areas are larger or have more members than others, so there may be one, two, or three members for them. At present the time served is three years, arranged in such a fashion that no area with more than one representative loses both together.

There are various other members plus the usual President, Vice-President, Chairman, Secretary and Treasurer.

The full Council meets twice a year; but the day-to-day affairs are run by an Executive Committee of five, elected from among Council members.

DISTRICT ADVISERS

These are appointed by the Council from time to time, in different parts of the country. They are experienced fanciers and able to give advice. They can be very useful to the novice, as it means there is usually someone fairly near at hand, to whom they can take their problems.

The Council keeps a register of these names and publishes them in their Book of Rules and Regulations, which you receive on joining.

INVESTIGATION COMMITTEE

This is a small committee, which deals with complaints and reports of misconduct. After hearing a case, a decision is made and if the charge is found to be justified, a penalty is imposed which can extend between a fine to suspension for a given period or life. An appeal can be made, which is heard by the Executive and they have the power to reverse the decision.

THE LIBRARY

The B.R.C. has an extensive library of books, both modern and old, some volumes of great interest going back to the very early days of the Fancy's existence. These can be borrowed for the price of the return postage. Also, any member is welcome to drop in at the headquarters at any time, to look round and seek advice or just to sit and browse through the books.

SHOWS

Star grading is awarded to shows from small one star right up through two, three and five star status. There are many cups to be won at the major shows and Breed Challenge certificates are given at all star shows, which count towards British Rabbit Council Championships.

All these details and many others will be found in the book of Rules and Regulations and other literature that you will receive when you join.

This is only a very brief summary of its activities, but sufficient to show you why you should join as soon as possible.

ADDRESS

The address of the British Rabbit Council offices is Purefoy House, 7, Kirkgate, Newark, Nottinghamshire.

THE NATIONAL NETHERLAND DWARF CLUB

This is the club which caters exclusively for the Netherland Dwarf. You will be wise to join it early; apart from all the help you will receive from it, there are many Cups, Championships and Diplomas to be won. They are naturally confined to members. The current address can be obtained from the British Rabbit Council (changes on annual basis).

There is also a Panel of Specialist judges, people with particular knowledge of the Dwarf. These are elected annually by the members of the Club. Only they can award the Netherland Dwarf Club certificates that count towards making a Club Champion.

The Club has its own special rules and runs special shows during the year, awarding its major trophies to the winners of various classes. Judges for these shows **must** be on the special Panel.

There are Area clubs, too. It is not compulsory to join these, if you do not wish; but it is advisable, because you will then have access to other breeders of Dwarfs near where you live. They put on their own shows in their Areas and award their own Trophies during the year. The address of your Area secretary can be obtained from the National Secretary.

The National Netherland Dwarf Club is, at the time of writing, one of the largest in the country and has many members from other countries, too. Many of these correspond with the British members and even visit them.

It is in your best interests to join the National Club, as soon as you are sure that this is the breed for you. The Secretary is in touch with members and can often help in the matter of where stock is available at a given time, and who might be a good person to advise you.

I. Kleurdwerg's Steel Buck. (Courtesy of J. Van Riesen. Photo by C. Aalbers. Holland)

CHAPTER 10

The Healthy Dwarf

SIGNS OF HEALTH

What should the really healthy Dwarf look like? Just a few words on this for the beginner.

Whenever the rabbitry is visited, all the stock should look alert, bright of eye and interested in whatever they are doing. Even a resting or sleeping Dwarf should still look healthy. It will probably awake, when spoken to, and sit up smartly. The eye must be bright and clear, no suspicion of dampness, much less of watering.

'WET EYE'

It is most important to check the stock every single day for any signs of 'wet eye'. It may be only the start of a cold, which will clear up (perhaps the hutch is in a draught), in which case, move it; or it can be the first signs of a disease much feared and very difficult, often impossible, to cure. If the latter is the case, the earlier it is found, the earlier treatment can begin; that is, if an attempt to do so is to be made; but more about that later.

NOSE AND GENITALS

Look daily at the nose, which should **not** be runny or wet. Inspect the genitals at least once a week. They should be clean with no discharge, no swellings; but remember, a doe might be in season, or coming into season, when this will be either swollen or swelling, and either purple or dark pink. This is perfectly normal.

NORMAL APPEARANCE

Your rabbits should appear pleased to see you, probably come to the front of their hutches. Get to know the different habits of each individual rabbit for a good, observant stockman senses at once if anything is amiss. Use eyes and senses and this instinct will gradually develop.

Has each one cleared up its food well? Are they all drinking their usual amounts of water? If one is drinking an abnormal amount, watch it extra carefully that day. It can be the first signs of serious trouble.

NORMAL EXCRETA

The normal motions (*faeces*) of a rabbit are formed and look like little dark pellets. As a rule, the rabbit uses only one corner for urine, so it is a simple thing to clean out just this one place daily. The 'pellets', however, will be scattered all over the floor.

CONDITION OF PAWS

In between the paws at the front should be dry. If they are wet, it has probably been rubbing or wiping a wet nose. Watch this condition carefully. The back legs, also, should be dry in the inner sides; although this is not always the case with stud bucks. When used regularly some tend to develop a dribble, or remain damp, even matted slightly, after mating does.

NORMAL COAT

A healthy rabbit washes itself regularly; they are very fastidious creatures and hate dirt on their bodies. The fur shines, it is not what is called 'staring', (i.e., looking rough, dull) and when a hand is run up from rump to neck, remains standing up and does not fall gently and easily back into place, as it should. It should feel soft, not harsh, to the touch.

NORMAL TEETH

Examine the teeth frequently. The thing to watch for is that all are growing straight. It is very easy to miss the fact that they are curving under and growing along the top of the soft palate (roof of the mouth). If not on the look out the animal will slowly become unable to eat properly and will go thin, by which time it is too late to take action.

Teeth can, of course, be cut, but it is not really worth while, because the problem is incurable, and the animal must *never* on any account be used for breeding, however many other good points it has. The teeth continue to grow crooked and the more they are cut the faster they grow. This means that it is kinder and wiser to steel the heart and put it down.

MOULT

This is usually obvious and shows itself in various ways in different animals. Any sudden change of temperature can start it off, at any time of the year.

Agricultural shows, where the animals are under canvas, are frequent places for premature moults. If it is a hot day the sun heats up the tents to a temperature much beyond the normal; this fact plus lack of moving air, and some exhibits will return home well and truly in the moult.

If present at the show, see that exhibits get water to drink, and that any possible flaps of the tent are raised or lowered, thus creating whatever moving currents of air are possible. This can help to ward off the trouble.

Sometimes the first indication of moult is the appearance on the skin of small blue patches, when the coat is blown or rolled back. It is not seen on the top at first. New breeders can be very frightened if they see this and are afraid their animal has contracted a skin disease. This is an entirely natural reaction for a beginner, but he will soon get to recognise the true problem.

Another form is a thin line appearing down one or both sides or flanks. It looks like a dividing line. The rabbit can usually go on showing for a short time until it becomes too obvious. If the rabbit is a particularly good one, most judges will allow a little latitude in this. However do not bank on it, as some judges will not tolerate moult at any stage. It is a case of getting to know individual judges' likes and dislikes. 'Horses for courses' applies in the Fancy, just as anywhere else.

Some show early signs of moult by a small patch beginning in and around the nose. This is one of the commonest places for it to start. Another is just around the rump, spreading slowly up the flanks. (Incidentally, this is often one of the last places to clear.) When fully in moult, the rabbit will look exactly like a 'ragbag'. The quicker and heavier the moult comes, usually the quicker it is in clearing.

99

Some of the shaded colours look worst, and take longest to clear, appearing to have a patchy type of moult. That is, they are all different shades of colours all over, instead of saddles shading nicely down.

BREEDING AND MOULT

Sometimes a rabbit appears to be constantly moulting, starting again as soon as one has finished. This is obviously not going to be any use for anything, especially breeding. There is a need to keep a close watch on any near relations. Is it a family inheritance? If it seems that a number of relations are doing it, then it is inbred into the strain. Either get rid of the lot and start again, or try to breed it out.

The correct approach is to dispose of that particular animal, then be extra careful to mate together only **distant** relations of that strain. Time **may** breed it out, but it would probably take far longer than it is worth. If this problem ever arises, make a quick decision and do not delay in carrying it out.

HELP WITH MOULT

Can anything be done to help through moult? Yes. Although a natural process, it does impose a certain amount of strain on the animal. Give adequate rations, a good nourishing diet, with plenty of protein.

Groundsel is a helpful wild green plant and usually enjoyed. It does have some good effect on moult, but do remember that it is also a laxative, so if stock is not used to greenfood, feed it sparingly and watchfully, and only in very small quantities.

Every day, take the moulters out and groom them. Spit on each palm of the hands, rub them together lightly then begin to smooth the rabbit from nape to rump. Put added pressure on gradually, until the coat is being stroked quite firmly. This will help to remove all those loosened hairs, thus allowing the new coat to come through. If left to nature the loose hairs will, of course, drop out in good time, but they are hindering the new ones getting through.

A common comment to be seen in judges' reports is 'in two coats today', or 'in too many coats today to do much with'. A little time spent helping the old coat out and the new one in, is to groom away with hands and spit. Spit also puts a nice gloss on a coat, and is not to be despised in show preparation.

CHAPTER 11

Sickness and Disease

The Dwarf is difficult in disease although no more delicate or prone to illness than other breeds. It is perfectly hardy, but when it does go sick its organs are so tiny, in comparison with other breeds, that it has not a great deal with which to fight.

All miniatures succumb quicker to disease by their very nature. Also, the Dwarf is not a 'natural' rabbit, but a 'made' one and highly inbred. Open up a New Zealand Red, a Beveren, a Satin and then a Dwarf. Observe the tiny kidneys and small abdomen, the minute heart and lungs in comparison. It will readily be understood why any inflammation of intestines or lungs, or strain on the heart, is more likely to be fatal.

Never breed with anything unhealthy, however good its type. This will only cause endless future trouble. Prevention is better than any cure. It is not worth trying to cure the illness unless it is a very simple one, the animal valuable in some special respect, and the sickness has been discovered and diagnosed early.

UNDERLYING DISEASES

Some illnesses are really signs and symptoms of an underlying disease; it is much more important to pinpoint the disease, than to cure the particular animal's apparent symptoms.

The most usual illnesses are **Blows, Scours**, and in the case of suckling does and half grown youngsters, **Pneumonia** and **Bronchitis**.

ACHIEVING PEAK CONDITION

It is, therefore, of prime importance to maintain every animal in peak condition. This is achieved by good husbandry, an accumulation of knowledge, a willingness to learn, a detailed knowledge of each individual's habits (so that anything unusual is noticed at once), an understanding of the principles concerning hygiene, scrupulous attention to detail, plus that little bit of instinct, flair, call it what you will, which all good stockmen possess or develop. A strong, healthy rabbit will usually make a quick recovery from minor illnesses.

SHOWS

One difficulty is the transmission in and out of the rabbitry of animals to and from shows. It is not possible to isolate each one every time it goes away, which would be ideal; so, be careful to inspect on return and for a day or two afterwards.

Fleas are a great spreader of disease and can easily be picked up at shows by close contact on the judging table. Mice are also spreaders (access to the rabbitry by the family pet cat might be considered).

GENERAL TREATMENT OF SICK RABBITS

Once a rabbit is sick, either remove it to the Sick Quarters, or, if it is too ill for that, isolate the best way possible. Thoroughly clean out and disinfect the hutch. Put in plenty of warm, dry bedding. Make sure it is well covered up at night, but that adequate air can reach it. Do not leave any spilled food on the floor.

Certain greenfoods have special medicinal properties (especially wild flowers); learn them by heart and try to have a supply at hand.

The rabbit is incapable of vomiting, so does not have this natural way of ridding itself of anything which has disagreed. This also applies to sweating, which makes it more vulnerable to heat exhaustion than other animals. Do not, therefore, allow hutches to be in full midday sun or heat. Make sure there is always a sufficient circulation of air in any enclosed quarters.

MOST COMMON AILMENTS

Only those most likely to affect the Dwarf are explained.

Abscess

Signs

Rabbit off colour while the abscess is developing, loss of appetite, then a lump under the skin can be felt. See if it feels soft and full of liquid, as opposed to hard. (In which case it is more likely to be a cyst and a case for the Veterinarian).

Treatment

Cut away the fur from round the lump, using a sterilised razor blade and make a quick incision. Wear rubber gloves and swab out the pus with gauze soaked in salt and water (or other disinfectant). Get it all out. This will need doing for several days, as more pus will form. On no account must healing be allowed to begin until the wound is completely clean and pus free. If it heals over the top, the hole underneath will only fill up again, as 'nature abhors a vacuum', and you will have to incise again. It must be allowed to heal from the *bottom* of the wound upwards. If, on cutting, it is *not* pus, but hard and solid, then it is definitely for the Veterinarian.

Blows Or Bloat

This can be diagnosed when the animal sits hunched up in a corner with eyes glazed and staring into space. If picked up the distended belly, full of fermenting gases, can be felt. The belly will sound hollow if tapped.

The rabbit cannot bring wind up or down, as does a dog, so gases go on fermenting and building up with no way to escape. It is essential to disperse them quickly. Often the trouble has progressed too far when found. Only a few things can be tried, so do be constantly on the watch for Blows in its early stages, when there is a chance of halting its progress.

Causes

Very probably greedy eating and drinking, particularly of fresh new greenstuff. It can also be caused by leaving the rabbit too long with nothing to eat and then overfeeding. So, if you have had to leave a rabbit unfed for some reason, go carefully and only feed a little at a time, until normal feeding can be resumed.

Treatment

First, give a saltspoonful of Bicarbonate of Soda (or better still Bi-So-Dol, proprietary brand) in a very little warm milk. (See method of administering medicine.) If the rabbit is not already too ill, the best and quickest thing, following this treatment, is exercise. Get it out of its hutch, away from other rabbits, and keep it moving. The sick rabbit is not going to want to do this, but be ruthless for it must be kept on the move. This approach can only be adopted if the trouble is found early and not too much damage has already occurred.

If successful, watch the diet very carefully in future, because it is

103

probably one with a weakness in its digestive system to some ingredient. The animal can take some rest in between bouts of running up and down, by being held, upside down, in your arms, and gently massaging the belly, thus trying to disperse the wind manually. Parents should be familiar with this movement, as it is the one used with small children that have wind or are constipated.

Another possible course is one used in hospitals to relieve wind, following abdominal operations; but it requires great care and a delicate sense of touch in such a small animal.

Get a very fine piece of surgical tubing, rubber or plastic, with a small bore. You will need a small bowl of water, also. Grease the end of the tubing well, then very gently pass it up the rabbit's anus (back passage). Place the other end, which is also open, in the bowl of water. If bubbles appear on the surface, the gases are escaping and you can continue until no more bubbles come up. If nothing happens, abandon the trial.

Enema

The next method is an exercise not without danger in inexperienced hands; but it is not difficult to learn. It must be done with great caution, but it can work well. It is the **Enema**.

Very similar equipment is needed, a bowl of water, only warm and soapy this time. Use a very bland soap; in fact, that old-fashioned soft green soap used years ago is just right, if obtainable.

For dealing with Dwarfs, only a very small syringe must be used, a fountain pen filler or an eye or ear dropper is ideal. Fill it with the soapy mixture and gently introduce it up the back passage; expel the contents *very* gently and withdraw the syringe. Make sure you expel all air from the syringe each time before putting in more solution. Do not keep putting more and more fluid in unless what has already gone in is being returned. If nothing comes back after, say, three syringes full, stop at once. The idea is to get the rabbit to pass some form of motion, or even the solution, and with it the wind will come away. Whatever the results, the water must be returned. If this does not occur *stop* the treatment.

Constipation

This is detected either by the pellets passed being either small, abnormally hard or scanty. The animal can sometimes be seen straining to pass them with no result.

Treatment

Give extra water to drink with a pinch of Epsom salts in it, plus a good helping of laxative greenfood, mixed if possible, to loosen the motion. If these fail an enema, as previously described, can be tried; use about half a tea cup of bland soapy water. If available, dandelion in moderation is excellent. Some small piece of root vegetable, such as carrot, may help. Withhold some of the pellet feeding and give only a little plus the greenfood, until normal motions begin.

Colds

A cold begins with the animal sneezing, progressing on to difficult breathing and runny nose or blocked nose. It must be treated with complete urgency, because the symptoms are similar to 'Snuffles', a very serious disease indeed, usually entailing the destruction of the stock.

Treatment

At the first signs of a cold, isolate the animal and watch to see if a thick, yellowy discharge starts from the nose. If it is only blocked, or a clear, watery one, then it is probably only a cold. Keep the animal warm with extra hay and bedding. Wipe away all discharge from eyes and nose as often as possible (wear gloves). Smear a little Camphorated oil, oil of Eucalyptus or *Vick* on the hutch walls to ease the breathing. This can be placed in its travelling box for a period, with the oils smeared on the walls — not too much, as either oil is rather strong. The rabbit should recover in a few days.

Chills
Causes

Usually not sufficient bedding; allowing the bedding to remain wet and unchanged too long; hutches exposed to damp, rain and draughts.

Treatment

Correct the causes. Add extra bedding, remove from cold or draughty place, make sure it is warm and dry. Give nourishing food. (See further under chapter on Bedding.)

Convulsions

Causes

Occasionally found in youngsters by overheating. It can happen in adults also. It could be the onset of fits. In an adult, which has never had a convulsion before, look for a possible outside cause before destroying. Is the weather unduly hot? Is the hutch in full heat causing an airless position?

Administering eye drops.

Wrong

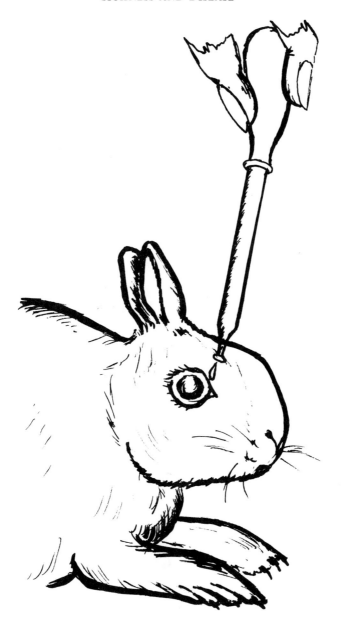

Wrong

Correct

Treatment

Remove to a cool and darkened place and keep it quiet. On no account allow any sudden noises near the animal as this will trigger off another fit. See that it has water to drink, preferably from a bottle. Crush an aspirin to powder and give some. Remove all pots and articles that might injure it. Leave it alone, but if the fit recurs kill the rabbit for it will pass on the weakness.

Cannibalism

See chapter on Breeding.

Conjunctivitis

This is a painful eye disease. The eye appears red, swollen and inflamed. Light appears to hurt it and will be avoided.

Causes

These are various. The trouble sometimes comes with a cold. Most often it is some form of irritation. Often a virus may be the cause.

Treatment

Drops or ointment will ease it. Aureomycin ointments will have to be prescribed, but *Golden Eye* ointment can still be obtained and usually is successful, unless it is a virus case.

Sticky Eye

A 'sticky eye' or a discharging one should be watched carefully, because it could be the first sign of serious trouble. Either way, it will need bathing to get it open. This will probably have to be done twice or three times a day. Use warm milk and water or warm water, with a salt-spoon of salt added. Bathe gently to remove the sticky matter and use a fresh piece of material for each eye and for each stroke, in case it is infectious — working from the inner corner to the outer corner. Finish one eye before starting on the other, if both are affected.

A smear of *Golden Eye* ointment along the inside of the lower lid will help to ease the inflammation and give comfort.

Coccidiosis

This is one of the biggest killers and most feared. It is extremely catching and spreads rapidly. Many rabbits have a mild form of it and suffer no serious setbacks, but they can spread it, so are always a danger. When discovered, it is often too late to effect a cure.

For most rabbit ailments the operative word is very definitely **pre-**

vention. By the end of this book, this word, if no other, should have made some impression. This is more true of coccidiosis than almost any disease.

One of the best ways of prevention, or to minimise an attack, is to feed an added coccidiostat to the food of the young. More can be read about this in the chapter on Breeding and Feeding of the young. Because of this, much of this dreaded disease is not seen today. It is almost impossible to cure, if well established, partly because it is almost impossible to fulfil the necessary treatment completely.

What Is Coccidiosis?

The reader should try to understand a little about the disease in order to appreciate the care needed in both prevention and cure.

Causes

It is caused by a parasite, which attacks the intestines (guts) usually, though it can also attack the liver. It is passed out through the anus with the droppings, scattered over the hutch floor. Thus, it is impossible to prevent the animal ingesting them again. So a vicious circle is set up. The re-ingested parasites reattack the gut, the parasites hatch out, live for a time on the gut, then are passed out to be re-ingested once more.

This is only a much simplified version because the whole process is much more complicated. Obviously, while the parasites lie in the hutch on the floor, there is also a problem of spreading by flies and insects.

Signs of Coccidiosis

Signs are a harsh staring coat, the usual huddled up appearance associated with sick rabbits, plus rapid weight loss and condition. No amount of food taken makes any difference to this loss of weight.

If several are affected, it is worth killing one and opening it up. The tell tale signs will be obvious. It is common to find the intestines and/or liver covered in a number of white (occasionally yellow) spots.

Post-mortem

Should any animal die of an unknown cause, always carry out a post-mortem. Apart from finding the probable cause of death, protection can be started for the remaining stock should early evidence of coccidiosis be found.

Treatment

'**Embazin**' solution should be added to the drinking water of all stock at once. This is a solution of a specific drug made up into a solu-

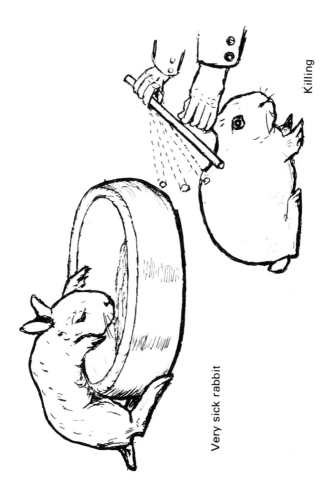

Killing

Very sick rabbit

Killing, probably only solution. (Sharp blow behind ears, on neck with heavy, iron instrument probably quickest and kindest).

tion by May and Baker and can be bought in quantity. It can be added to drinking water all the time, if wished, as a preventative.

Obviously greenfood and other food spilt will become infected. The rabbit passes the eggs in the first stages, so it is hopeless trying to keep the floor clear of them. All food must be given by a system which will achieve this as far as possible. Wasted food must be removed quickly. Cleaning out must be frequent and all bedding burnt. Call in the Veterinarian for advice.

Isolate all sick immediately. When cleaning out, use ammonia in the water. This is the only known disinfectant of any use against this particular disease. Wear gloves all the time when attending to stock.

Dealing With Infected Hutches

When a hutch is finished with, either burn it, or if you must use it again, scrub thoroughly with hot water and ammonia and go over it with a blow lamp. Leave it outside in the air and/or sunlight. Afterwards repaint both inside and outside and leave it as long as possible before using again.

This is really a disease where it is wisest to kill immediately following a diagnosis. Certainly never use one that has recovered for breeding.

Canker

This is not uncommon in rabbits, but it rarely affects the Dwarf. However, the odd case does crop up.

Causes

A small mite sets up an irritation deep inside the ear. The animal scratches more or less continuously and the interior becomes very inflamed. Wax often forms.

Signs

The first sign is often the rabbit shaking its head and holding it over on the affected side.

Wax can often be seen inside. It may be loose and offensive smelling or it may be hard and encrusted. You can be fairly sure the rabbit has had it for some considerable time, as it starts deep inside the ear. It is highly infectious, because the rabbit will shake its head a lot, thus throwing out little blobs of infected wax everywhere.

As well as treating the animal, inspect all other stock in close proximity. It may well have picked it up at a show. This is one of the risks run. This is an added reason for so much regular inspection of stock.

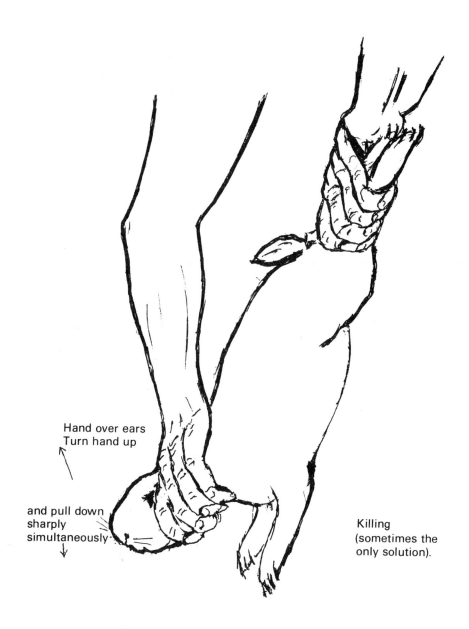

Hand over ears
Turn hand up

and pull down
sharply
simultaneously

Killing
(sometimes the
only solution).

Fortunately it is reasonably easy to effect a cure, but a rabbit that develops this trouble, will always be susceptible to it to some extent.

Treatment
The cure is to get rid of the wax manually, first, then kill the mites. For two or three days, put three or four drops of warmed oil in the affected ear, night and morning. Then, when the wax seems reasonably soft, wrap the rabbit up in a piece of sacking or old blanket, with its head poking out. With cotton wool wrapped round a small stick (Johnson's Baby Buds are ideal), soak this in peroxide of hydrogen and water mixed and *gently* remove the wax and crusts, which have softened up. Keep changing the wool and burn after use. When satisfied that no more can be done that day — remember everything cannot be removed at once, because of the possibility of further inflaming the tender ear — repeat the oil procedure again for two days and continue removing the softened wax.

When the ear is clear, pop inside a couple of drops of **Benzyl Benzoate** (no more for a Dwarf). This is an old and tried method of dog breeders. It should kill the 'mites' should any remain. After this, puff some proprietary powder for canker in the ear once a month as a routine. Once an animal has had this problem, it is likely to return. Powdered Flowers of Sulphur are equally suitable.

Diarrhoea

See Scours.

Eyes

There are one or two eye problems, some serious and some not so serious. It is important to distinguish between the two. Under this heading, see also **Conjunctivitis**, which is an eye condition dealt with under its own heading.

Foreign Body in Eye
Cause, usually sawdust or hay or straw; could be a speck of dust flown in.

Treatment
See if you can see anything first which may be quite easy to remove. If not, it may be necessary to evert the eyelids to carry out a proper examination. Do not attempt to do this unless experienced or under supervision. It is not difficult, but can be dangerous in inexperienced hands.

114

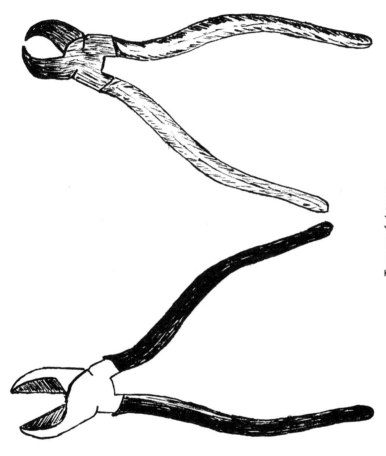

Two useful types
of toenail cutters
Do **not** cut into
the blood line

Method

The method is to get a very small piece of wood (in humans, a matchstick is used, so this gives some idea of the size). Help will almost certainly be needed to hold the animal, as it will object strongly. Place the wood along the eyelid just near the eyelashes, outside, and gently roll the eyelid back over the wood. Remember the animal can easily be blinded, if this is not done with the utmost care. If there are any struggles on the part of the animal release it immediately, wait, and start again. If the offending article can be seen, remove it.

This is best done by the same method as with humans. Wet the corner of a soft handkerchief, twist tightly, and flick gently. The hankie is firm enough for the job, yet soft. If the offending body can be seen, but cannot be removed, put an antibiotic ointment or drops in the eye three times daily, thus trying to flush it out, at the same time keeping infection at bay.

Some Causes Other Than Foreign Body

Is it in a draught? Was the outside rabbitry covered up last night? Think of all the simple things first and take suitable action.

If none of these, then the task becomes more difficult, because genuine eye illnesses are not easy to cure. Some stud bucks develop it after being used at stud.

There are various eye drops on the market, plus a fair number of ointments. **Albucid**, sulphacetamide sodium, is a favourite with Veterinarians. Many fanciers have found it excellent. It is most used against 'wet eye'.

Ocusol

Sulphacetamide sodium plus zinc sulphate, used for superficial infections and irritations.

Framygen

Framecetine sulphate, for very simple eye infections, comes in drops or ointment.

Chloromycetine, Chloramphenical

Very good indeed for bacterial conjunctivitis or serious eye infections, in ointment or drops. A veterinarian's prescription is needed for some of these. An old fashioned remedy, *Golden Eye* ointment, is good for almost anything and freely available over the counter.

One drop (for Dwarfs) three times daily is usual. Do not miss a single dose. It is usually supplied with a dropper, but do make sure of this before leaving the chemist. If not, buy a dropper.

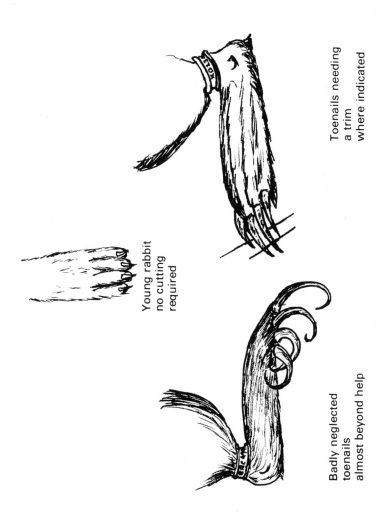

Toenails needing
a trim
where indicated

Young rabbit
no cutting
required

Badly neglected
toenails
almost beyond help

How to apply Drops or Ointment

There is a right and wrong way of applying drops which is connected with the anatomy of the eye. The treatment is no use if done wrongly.

For drops, pull up a few drops in the dropper — more than you need, as it may not go in first attempt. With the rabbit sitting on the table, side ways on, put your hand firmly on its head, drawing it back slightly. Move the thumb forward onto the top eyelid and open the eye as far as possible. With the other hand, release two drops into the inner corner. If it trickles out, repeat. The rabbit will blink and so distribute the fluid across the eye. Never on any account must you drop it directly on the pupil, and always the inner corner.

For an ointment (which is easier), hold the rabbit firmly the same way, except that the thumb, or finger, whichever is easier, is on the *lower* lid. Again, working from the inner corner, draw the lower lid down and squeeze the tube along the inside of the bottom lid towards the outer corner. This should leave a smear of ointment along the inside. The whole thing must be carried out as fast as possible, because the rabbit is not going to sit there docilely when it realises what is happening. If you can get assistance to hold the animal it is better.

Watch others carry out the treatment several times before you try it, and have help for the first time or two. It is quite easily mastered, and a very useful thing to be able to do.

Ointment is preferable to drops when possible, because of the certainty of getting at least some in the right place.

Heat Exhaustion

Prevention, as advised in other chapters, should come first. Make sure all the proper precautions have been taken.

Causes

Obviously one cannot control the weather, and cases occur at Agricultural shows, where the heat builds up under the canvas and there is little free passage of air. Should a case occur at home, remove the animal to the shade and cool as quickly as possible. Remove all hay or straw bedding. Wring out a cloth in cold water and lie the animal on it on the hutch floor. Ensure good air circulation.

Leave it as quiet as possible. Sluice down the outsides and roof of the hutch. Do this as often as possible to reduce the inside temperature. If you have a deep freeze, keep a brick in it. Place this in the hutch. If you have no deep freeze, a bottle of water can be kept in the fridge. This is not so good, as it does not retain the cold for as long, but it is better than nothing. If the animal is very badly affected, wrap the rabbit up in a cloth rung out in cold water.

When it appears to be coming back to normal, replace the bedding slowly, a little at a time, so that it does not catch a chill. Be sure it is warm and inside for the night. Remove solid food until a desire to eat is shown.

Enteritis

This is one of the worst things to encounter. Almost nothing can be done. It is often mistaken for Blows in the early stages, as the early symptoms are similar. The rabbit, however, has an excessive thirst and, in the Dwarf, will often be found hanging over or in the water pot in obvious distress, with eyes glazed in the later stages.

Usually it is a waste of time trying to effect a cure. The injections are expensive and a lot of damage has been done. If the rabbit recovers, it never reverts to its former self and must on no account be used for breeding.

There is a school of thought that thinks this may be an inherited or transmitted disease. In any case, it will always be a delicate animal, needing constant watching. Once it is a definite diagnosis, it is kinder and safer to kill it. Burn all bedding and thoroughly disinfect the hutch.

Impaction

This is retained pellets or faeces, that the rabbit has not been able to pass, and is more serious than constipation. If not remedied quickly, obstruction will occur.

Treatment

Try a good mixture of greenfoods first, particularly the laxative varieties and avoid those used to combat Diarrhoea. In severe cases give a saltspoonful of Epsom salts in a dessertspoon of warm water. If this does not work, give half a teaspoonful of liquid paraffin. As a last resort, give a soapy enema as described under Constipation.

Cut down drastically on solid food and continue with well mixed greens until the motion return to normal. If the animal is valuable, see the Veterinarian.

Injuries

These are accidents such as fractures or accidental tearing of the skin or caused by falling out of the hutch.

Treatment

Fractures are obviously a case for the Veterinarian. It may mean the rabbit is no longer any good for show, but it does not impair its breeding value.

Tearing of the skin can happen in a variety of ways. A common one is leaving the litter too long on the doe. She becomes irritated and nips them, when they pester her. They may fight among each other, pulling out bits of fur, or scratching. The bucks will fight together or try to 'ride' the does. If the doe is not willing, he may try to hold her down, by grabbing at her fur on the neck or back.

All wounds require cleansing with normal saline solution, done regularly for several days while the skin is broken. The rabbit will almost certainly lick itself, if the wound is in an accessible place.

Coloured Rabbits

These are difficult to deal with because if left to itself the wound will probably grow in white fur.

Treatment

One of those Old Wives' Tales has served well on occasions. It must be persevered with, however. Rub Vaseline in; rub it very thoroughly until you are sure you have got plenty well in. The rabbit is assuredly going to lick itself, as soon as possible and so, remove most of what lies on top. This is why it must be done at least three times a day.

Continue until the new fur starts coming in. When this happens, with luck, it will be coloured. As soon as the bare patch is completely covered, it can be left, knowing that it will continue to grow longer and retain its colour. This *does* work and with a valuable show exhibit, it is well worth the trouble.

Injuries of this sort, resulting in loss of colour, do not affect a rabbit for breeding purposes.

Friars Balsam is a reliable antiseptic; but not on white rabbits, it stains.

Myxomatosis

Cause

A particular flea carried by the rabbit and passed on by direct contact; e.g.; mating, at shows, or by mosquitoes and insects from infected rabbits.

Signs

Off food, a large, misshapen, lumpy head appearing; appears 'dazed'.

Plate 6
Top: Mr. D. Pepper's Otter
Bottom: Mr. P. Ralph's Fawn Netherland Dwarf and Dwarf Lop. (Note different ear carriage).

Plate 7

Top Left: Woody Night Shade

Bottom Left: Deadly Nightshade *(Atropa belladonna)* up to 90cm. high. The colour of the flowers and the following dark berry like seeds are very distinctive.

Top;   Hemlock *(Conium maculatum)* up to 180cm. high. Smooth round stems with brownish purple spots.

Bottom: Fools Parsley *(Aethusa cynapium)* about 100cm. high with a pronounced "beard" of bracts below the flowers.

Treatment

Best to kill the affected animal at once. Send for the Veterinarian to vaccinate all remaining stock. There is a satisfactory vaccine now. It would be wise to vaccinate annually as routine, if living in an area where it is prevalent, or at the first appearance of the disease in a wild rabbit. Experienced fanciers can get the vaccine and use it, but beginners should not attempt the cure.

Off Colour or Listless and Not Eating

A rabbit, like any human being, is sometimes off colour; not particularly ill, but out of sorts.

Signs

Looks like what is called in a child 'run down'. Listless, gone off its feed and not showing much interest in what is going on.

Treatment

Provided no real illness is present, resort to grandmother's remedy, **Parrish's Food**. Younger members reading this, may not have heard of it. Go to a chemist. It is a syrupy liquid in a bottle. Put two teaspoonfuls in a six ounce drinking bottle. It can be seen if the rabbit is taking it and how much. This is the advantage of rearing rabbits from the beginning on drinking bottles, rather than dishes. This is a fine tonic and highly efficacious. Give as much hay as will be consumed.

Pneumonia

Usually this is fatal — usually fast.

Signs

The rabbit has a temperature and difficulty in breathing, which is shallow and much increased in rate. Because there is some watering of the eyes, it is left too late, having been mistaken for the early stages of a cold. The animal will not eat and rapidly becomes very ill indeed. Some dribbling at the mouth may be present.

There is nothing at the time of writing to be done, except to ensure it is not in a draught and is warm and dry. If spotted early and not too far progressed, a Veterinarian may save the rabbit.

Poisons

There are a large number of these, but not all apply to Dwarfs. The eating of poisonous greenstuffs is one that should never occur. Familiarise yourself with them early on. Pictures or descriptions are given in the appropriate chapter.

Causes

The biggest danger lies at Agricultural Shows. Here is where, unknown to anyone, a visitor, especially a child, has picked up a handful of grass, or suchlike, from the dirty floor and pushed it in the cage. The rabbit may recover, but there is very little one can do about it, because one seldom knows it has happened, or it is too late by the time the rabbit arrives home and is seen to be unwell.

Another cause, though not so common, is creosote or paint poisoning. If creosote is used *inside* the hutches as well as outside, then sufficient time *must* be allowed for it to be absorbed and to dry out thoroughly. Too much haste in putting stock in a hutch can be disastrous. If used the lead content of paint should be ascertained, as lead is a killer which should be avoided. Whitewash is much safer, better, cheaper and easily done over frequently, giving less chance for disease to take hold.

Oats and cereals have sometimes been sprayed, so do not be afraid to ask, when buying.

It is sometimes necessary to put down rat or mouse poison. Take care that it is well away from stock. If hutches do not have a sufficiently small mesh to prevent mice entering and carrying the poison on their feet then cover up the fronts.

Treatment

Usually the animal is dead when you find it. Precautions for the remaining stock is the answer.

Paralysis

This is usually paralysis of the hindquarters. Rarely the problem is caused by a brain tumour, for which nothing can be done.

Causes

Only those concerning Dwarfs need be considered. It occurs occasionally in a doe towards the end of rearing a litter. Do not leave too many young with a doe and do not leave them too long. Do not let a rabbit get constipated and strain itself. Do be watchful concerning litter boards and nesting boxes. If a doe is startled while feeding young, she may jump suddenly. If a nesting box is being used to confine the babies, she can actually fracture her spine. This is, of course, incurable. Occasionally it is the result of chill, in which case ensure warmth and comfort and see if this will do the trick. Sometimes, there is no apparent reason.

Thermometers

Right Type

Wrong Type

There is a method, but it is very time consuming, not guaranteed to work, and has to be persevered with over a considerable time. As the rabbit will be fit only for show afterwards and never for breeding, plus the trouble is likely to recur, decide first whether it is worth trying to save. It *may* choose to recur on the show table, so take this into consideration. If it has been caused by stress, then show conditions are the most likely to produce it again.

Treatment

For those who want to try the remedy here it is. However, let it be understood that this is in serious paralysis, because if it is only a mild form, more like a weakness of the hindquarters, then the Veterinarian may be able to give injections, if taken immediately.

Purchase a bottle of **syrup of hypophosphytes** (not to be confused with Hypophosphates from the chemist, plus a dropper. Give two drops three times daily. There is seldom any difficulty about this, as the rabbits usually like its sweet syrupy taste. Bring the rabbit indoors and place it in a comfortable box with high sides. Lie the rabbit on its side at first, on plenty of hay, with something absorbent underneath. It will have to be handfed, as it can not stand up.

Let it have some greenfood, as constipation must be avoided at all costs. Choose those which are laxative and also nourishing, including some that are titbits to tempt the appetite. Leave plenty of hay within reach for eating. Give water to drink, from a bottle if possible.

It will continue to pass pellets, so its position must be changed constantly, as it must not lie in its own excrement, nor the limbs allowed to become stiff. The rabbit is a very fastidious creature and this one will be helpless and completely dependent on you. Good hygiene is essential for its recovery and happiness. This will mean a lot of work, as a rabbit passes pellets fairly continuously.

It is a slow business, but if after a few days the patient is trying to get on its stomach, it is improving and it can try lying in a more natural position. Turn it over. If it cannot stay on its stomach, but keeps falling back, then lie it on its side again for a few more days, changing the position constantly. Presently it will remain in the more normal position.

The next step to watch for is when it tries to drag itself along. Don't encourage this too soon, not until its strength has been built up, although it can be regarded as a good sign.

The paralysis is likely to happen again without warning, so it is only worth all this work if it will be regarded as a family pet in future. Never on any account breed with it.

It is a treatment that does work quite often, so weigh up the pros and cons. The trouble may be for nothing.

Red Water

This complaint is quite common, but fortunately quite easy to cure. It is *not*, however, something that *should* be found in well run rabbitries.

Causes

Most frequently, the leaving of the rabbit in damp conditions, wet bedding, or windy places. The animal gets a form of cystitis, which is extremely painful, and can become serious if not dealt with at once.

Treatment

The cure should be obvious. Clean out the wet bedding and replace with a good depth of sawdust and plenty of warm hay. Ensure the hutch is in no draughts and is cosy. Give plenty to drink so the urine is not allowed to become concentrated and painful to pass. If this happens, the animal will be unable to pass it for pain and kidney problems will not be far away.

If the trouble does not clear up quickly, with simple treatment, take it to the Veterinarian.

Scours (Diarrhoea)

This is a very troublesome and frequent disease. It can be very serious or just a passing upset. It should never be taken lightly or neglected.

Signs

The rabbit passes runny, loose motions, with no resemblance to pellets. It looks miserable and lethargic. It does not eat.

Causes

This is usually a dietary upset. Has the rabbit been away from home for any reason? A show? One sometimes finds that some misguided person has put a large piece of roots or greenfood in the travelling box, when boxing it for the return journey. Sometimes greenfoods are fed at the show, though this is becoming increasingly unusual, due to pellet feeding being so common among breeders. Shows appear to stick to the safer oats. Has it been away for mating? Have visitors, particularly children, been visiting your rabbitry? Or has it just gorged itself?

Treatment

Feed a good mixed greenfood diet, consisting of a few choice things to tempt the appetite, and a very large proportion of the anti-scours varieties. The best are strawberry, raspberry, and blackberry leaves. Shepherds' purse is a tonic as well as an astringent. Consult the chapter on wildfoods for the best mixture. This is why it is so important to collect these in season and keep a big supply dried off for winter use. If obtainable put a few drops of chlorodyne in the drinking water.

Mix some powdered chalk, obtainable from the chemist, or some kaolin to a paste with a very little water; put it in a teaspoon and push it in the rabbit's mouth three times a day. This is quite safe, so a good teaspoonful will do no harm. If the rabbit struggles, get whatever you can in. Do not force the animal. Plaster the remainder around its nose and mouth area with your fingers or the spoon. Even when sick, the animal will always attempt to clean its face, thus getting quite a fair amount of the required medicine in this manner. If a rabbit makes no effort to clean itself, it is probably too far gone to make a reasonable recovery and it is better to kill it before it suffers more. Kaolin and morphine is much stronger, but needs a Vet's prescription. Try and get some from him to keep handy, because you are probably going to need it when he is not available; e.g., a weekend.

Keep the hutch and bedding as clean as possible and give plenty of hay.

Very Mild Scours

This is quite different and is usually a very mild digestive upset. Sometimes it is a form of stress.

Treatment

Clean the animal up with warm water as well as possible. Clean out the hutch, removing soiled bedding and add fresh material as often as necessary.

Feed plenty of anti-scours greenfood, dry crusts and reduce the pellet allowance drastically until recovery. Put a few drops of chlorodyne in the drinking water, if obtainable (see, also, 'Simple Homemade Diarrhoea Mixture' at end of this chapter).

The rabbit should return to normal within about forty-eight to seventy two hours. If not, suspect something more serious.

Snuffles

This is perhaps the most dreaded disease of all. It is not a killer, but it is highly infectious and almost impossible to effect a hundred per cent certain cure. The rabbit may *appear* to have recovered, but it will always be a carrier. It must never be used for breeding.

Signs

The first signs to appear are usually a little loss of condition, followed by sneezing. Watch any rabbit that sneezes, as it is so easy to mistake it for the common cold. Watch it closely if it has been to a show, or is new stock.

An ordinary cold may, or may not, be accompanied by a nasal discharge, but if there is one, it will be of a watery nature.

In Snuffles, it is thick, yellowy in colour and very sticky, it will cause distress to the animal, getting on its paws, and inside its front feet, where it has been rubbing its nose.

No matter how slight the attack, destroy the animal with all speed. Clean out, disinfect, and repaint the hutch, having moved it away from the rabbitry. If money permits, burn the hutch, along with the soiled bedding. Don't even attempt to cure the animal, as it is only inviting the spread of the disease round the rabbitry.

Teeth

The most usual problem is **Malocclusion** or crooked growth. This may be the result of an injury to the jaw or teeth, which will not preclude it from breeding, though it will ruin it for show. However, if it is not so caused, the kindest thing is to kill it. It consists of the front incisors growing inwards and backwards along the roof of the mouth (soft palate). These are the teeth with which the rabbit chops up its food, when it first enters the mouth. Without them, it is quite helpless. If not noticed in time (and it very seldom is), the rabbit becomes progressively thinner, loses condition, until finally it starves to death.

Treatment

If a decision to keep it has been taken, the teeth will have to be cut regularly. This is quite simple, but, unfortunately, the more you cut the faster the teeth grow. This is all that will be necessary to enable the rabbit to eat. Provided the animal is to be kept purely as a pet, do it by all means, using a pair of nail clippers, as shown, not scissors.

In Dwarfs, it is most important to include the teeth and mouth in the regular weekly inspection. It is an inherited weakness and can be passed on, so it is absolutely necessary to exclude it from all breeding plans, however excellent in other respects.

Toe Nails

The toe nails will grow too long from time to time and will require cutting. It is a normal thing and quite easy to manage.

Method

Have a pair of nail clippers — there is no need to go to the expense of veterinary ones — an ordinary pair, such as can be purchased at any chemist for human use, are adequate and about a third of the price.

It is best to learn how to do the job first. Take the rabbit along to an established breeder or adviser near by, and ask to be shown how it is done.

There is only one really important thing to learn; not to cut into the 'quick'. It will bleed badly, as well as frighten and hurt the rabbit. It is easy to see the right place in coloured rabbits. The end to be cut is white; look along the nail to the darker horn colour. In Dwarfs, about one eighth of an inch before the white meets the horn colour, cut firmly and quickly.

It is more difficult in white rabbits because there is no horn colour. Here you will find the white part changes to a pale pink. It is not easy to see without a little experience.

Toe nails must be kept properly cut. If not, they will curl round and dig into the skin.

Vent Disease

This is a nasty thing and can occur if all the proper precautions have not been taken. As its name suggests, it concerns the genitalia.

Methods

It can be introduced into a stud as the result of sending a doe away for mating, if the buck used is affected. An infected doe can come in for mating. (That is why it is very important to examine visiting does).

Signs

The vent will seem to have sores developing. These will eventually run into each other and possibly involve the anus (back passage). Scabs may appear round the nose and mouth from the animal's cleaning activities.

Treatment

Scrupulous cleanliness is the answer to prevention; but if a case does develop, mercurial ointment can be tried. Far, far better is to go straight to the Veterinarian for treatment. Isolate the animal. Wear rubber gloves when attending to it. Scrub both gloves and your hands every time. Remember the animal will lick itself, so continuous watch must be kept for the appearance of any sore round the mouth area.

Follow the Veterinarian's instructions to the letter. The disease can be cured. For inspecting a buck, don't forget to pull gently to expose the penis, as well as looking at the orifices and testicles.

Worms

There are several different kinds of these, each caused in a different way. The cure depends on which kind the animal has got. It is better to let the Veterinarian decide this until some years of experience have been gained. Again, wear gloves when attending to the animal.

If you want to try yourself to treat it, then RAL- EVAPO, a proprietary brand is an old and tested medicine. Be sure you say it is for a rabbit, because it is also used for dogs and other animals, in different forms. Remember to halve the dose, as it is for a Dwarf. It can be bought at most pet shops.

Prevention

This is the best cure. Constant care over feeding stuffs, make sure food cannot be run over by mice or rats and that your hay is safe from dog fouling. Dogs are great carriers of worms. This is one thing to bear in mind when deciding whether to feed wild greens. What animals run about from your proposed sites of gathering? Which diseases are they likely to carry? If used, as used it must be in some diseases, then make sure it is absolutely clean and well washed, both before use and before drying for store.

By now, it should be obvious to all that PREVENTION is the keyword to success in most aspects of the rabbit Fancy.

SOME USEFUL THINGS TO KEEP IN THE MEDICINE CUPBOARD

Aspirin Useful for fits, convulsions, heat stroke.
Albucid Eye drops. Sulphonamide drug.
Bi-So-Dol A proprietary brand medicine for indigestion, useful in a variety of alimentary tract upsets, including wind its early stages and diarrhoea if caused by dietary troubles.
Benzyl Benzoate Chemists will make up bottles. Good for external infestations and ear canker.
Calcium Carbonate (Powdered chalk) Good for diarrhoea and scours. Also for cleaning the coats of white rabbits.
Chlorodyne If obtainable. Good for diarrhoea and scours. (Used to be freely obtainable, now frequently requires a prescription).
Friars Balsam Can be used externally for applying to wounds. Do not use internally with Dwarfs.
Forceps Medical forceps, either Spencer Wells or Mosquitoes. More uses than any other piece of equipment. (Holding cotton wool

wrapped round them for swabbing wounds, cleaning out ears, pulling out splinters, etc.).

Golden Eye Ointment For most eye conditions, easy to apply. (Compounded of almond oil and glycerine, so very safe and soothing.)

Hydrogen Peroxide In a bottle, always dilute with water. For cleansing wounds and cleaning out ears in early cases of canker.

Izal Disinfectant for hutches.

Johnson's Baby Buds For cleaning eyes and ears. Particularly useful for Dwarfs.

Kaolin Powder Obtainable from chemist without prescription. For diarrhoea which is *not* scours, but a minor dietary upset.

Olive Oil For softening up wax in ears prior to removal.

Nail Clippers

Pair of Small Scissors

Parrish's Food In a bottle. Excellent tonic and aid to poor appetite.

Ral Evapo Proprietary brand; good for some types of worm infestation (important to say it is required for rabbits, as it is extensively used for many animals).

Sodium Chloride (common salt) Many uses. Keep a very large packet and make up a solution as required. Safe and easy to use. One teaspoon to half a pint of warm water.

Sodium Bicarbonate 0.9% eye lotion for 'sticky eye'.

Sodium Bicarbonate Ear Drops For cleansing dirty ears.

Sulphur Ointment For wounds or sore pads.

Syrup Of Hypophosphites For paralysis of hind quarters or back.

Roll of Cotton Wool

Roll of Narrow Bandage (For Dwarfs, ¼" - ½")

Rectal Thermometer Remember that an animal's temperature must always be taken rectally. This is one with a short end (usually blue) *not* the one with the long, thin silver end.

Vaseline For wounds, especially in coloured rabbits.

Simple Homemade Diarrhoea Mixture

NOTE: 3 - 6 grs. bicarbonate of bismuth mixed with 10 grs. of bicarbonate of soda.

Drop a little on the tongue twice daily.

CHAPTER 12

Beginners' Hints When First Entering Shows

There are a number of pitfalls in entering Shows. It is best to ask an experienced fancier of your local club to help with the entries and preparation.

LOCAL CLUB

It is most important to join the nearest club as soon as possible, because this is where your show career will begin, to where you can turn for help and guidance. In the smaller of the local shows, the rabbits can be sized up against reasonable competition and questions asked afterwards.

JUDGES AT SMALL SHOWS

Remember the judge may be a well known one, who is a member of the club and lives near, thus helping his club with expert knowledge at no great expense to the club. This is good. If he is a Dwarf Panel judge, don't hesitate to ask for his opinion of your rabbits afterwards.

On the other hand, the judge may be an experienced breeder only just venturing into judging via the small local shows. Even judges have to begin somewhere and learn their craft as they go along.

If he is a Dwarf breeder, you will probably get a reasonable placing of the Dwarfs. Do not get too upset if yours gets nowhere. He may not be too knowledgeable on Dwarfs, or there may be some very good specimens there on that day. At first always try to find out the reasons for the placings.

WHICH RABBITS AND HOW TO ENTER

A rabbit may *not* be entered that is not wearing a ring. The only exception to this being in 'Pets' or 'Condition Only' classes.

Complete the entry form in good time to avoid making hurried and, perhaps, unwise entries. This has to be dictated, to some extent, by cash available, as well as stock in show condition.

Study the schedule carefully. In early days, take it down to the rabbitry and examine it and stock together. This has another advantage for assessing of stock means that skill is being acquired which later means a valuable amount of information is already at hand for next year's matings.

Weaknesses are being stored in the memory to be improved, strong points are noted to be imprinted or strengthened. Also, a small step is being subconsciously taken towards judging stock and perhaps eventually becoming a judge. Time spent in the study of your stock is never wasted.

THE DWARF AS A SHOW BREED

The Dwarf is a good show rabbit. Breeds vary enormously in their lengths of show life. A number of breeds will only be fit to take major awards for one year in young classes and one year in adult ones. Some will have two years in adult classes. The Dwarf has a long show life, some colours considerably longer than others.

The **Red Eyed White** should show — and win — for a good five years.

The **Agouti** is about the same, but shows up more badly when in moult.

Blacks hold their type well, but can be difficult with colour, tending to go rusty, especially if exposed to sunlight. The same applies to **Sables** as regards fading (keep them out of strong sunlight), but they have a very useful show life.

The more delicate colours are not as long lasting, so if you have a good one and have had a couple or so of good show years from it, get it into the breeding pen.

LISTEN AND LEARN

Many views are held on every aspect of the Fancy, many arguments and discussions take place. They are the lifeblood of the Fancy. Listen to everything, try out what appeals to you, retain and discard according to your personal findings, experiment on your own later, and slowly evolve your own particular methods. **These will be right for you**.

SENDING OFF AND CHECKING IN OF STOCK

Send stock off in good time. If by rail, allow for delays. If by road, exactly the same; Saturdays and Sundays are a favourite for traffic diversions and heavy build ups. On arrival, check that everything has arrived, is properly penned and checked in. It is usually in order to pen your own stock, except at the very big shows, where appointed stewards do it. Still check that yours are in their correct pens. Mistakes happen.

Examine before penning for any stains that have got on during the journey.

HOW TO UNDERSTAND THE SCHEDULE

You must enter in the Breeds class first. If you do not so wish you need not enter any other.

BREED CLASSES

These are classes confined to a particular breed. They are divided into three sections, **Fancy breeds, Fur breeds**, and **Rex breeds**. The Netherland Dwarf is classed as a **Fancy breed**. There may be more than one class for some breeds, some may have special colour ones for their breeds.

DWARF CLASSES

There may well be several Dwarf classes. Choose the one with the right colour and the right age. If there is one for young or under 5 months, and yours is a youngster, this is its class. There may be classes for colours, for adults *and* youngsters, so do be very careful. See the following examples:

Any other colour or A.O.C. found in the separate breed sections means it is for the colours that have no special colour class of their own. This can be tricky until you are thoroughly familiar with procedures and why you should get expert help for some time when filling in entries. It is easy to confuse this description with, for instance, **Any Colour** OR A.C.

If there is no breed class, probably there are not enough Dwarfs in that area to warrant a special class for them. This does not mean you

* * TWO STAR OPEN SHOW * * AUGUST 3RD ONLY

Judges: R. Tribbeck Esq., Eastleigh, FANCY. J.K. Ward Esq., Leeds, FUR & REX.
Entry Fee — 10p. Prize Money — 50p, 30p and 20p. Guaranteed.

Class No.

315 Flemish, A.A.
316 Belgian Hare, A.A.
317 Dutch, B. or B. Adult
318 Dutch, B. or B. under 4 months
319 Dutch, A.O.C. Adult
320 Dutch, A.O.C. under 4 months
321 Netherland Dwarf White, A.A.
322 Netherland Dwarf White, under 5 months
323 Netherland Dwarf, A.O.C. Adult
324 Netherland Dwarf, A.O.C. under 5 months
325 English A.C., Adult
326 English A.C., under 5 months
327 Lop All Properties, A.A.
328 Silver A.C., A.A.
329 Tan, A.C. Adult
330 Tan, A.C. under 5 months
331 Polish, A.C. Adult
332 Polish, A.C. under 5 months
333 Himalayan, A.A.
334 Harlequin or Magpie Black, A.A.
335 Harlequin or Magpie, A.O.C., A.A.
336 A.O.V. Fancy, A.A.
337 Fancy Breeders, Adult (D)
338 Fancy Breeders, under 5 months (D)
339 Fancy Challenge, Adult (D)
340 Fancy Challenge, under 5 months (D)
341 Beveren White, Adult
342 Beveren White, under 5 months
343 Beveren A.O.C., Adult
344 Beveren A.O.C., under 5 months
345 Chinchilla Giganta, Adult
346 Chinchilla Giganta, under 5 months
347 N.Z. Red, Adult
348 N.Z. Red, under 5 months
349 N.Z. White, Adult
350 N.Z. White, under 5 months

Entry Fee 5p. Prize Money 25p, 15p, 10p

386 Junior Fancy
387 Junior Fur
388 Junior Rex
389 Junior Challenge (D)

Class No.

351 N.Z. Black, A.A.
352 Fox, A.C. Adult
353 Fox, A.C. under 5 months
354 Chinchilla, A.A.
355 Californian, Adult
356 Californian, under 5 months
357 Satin, A.C. Adult
358 Satin, A.C. under 5 months
359 A.O.V., Fur, A.A.
360 Fur Breeders, Adult (D)
361 Fur Breeders, under 5 months (D)
362 Fur Challenge, Adult (D)
363 Fur Challenge, under 5 months
364 Ermine, Adult
365 Ermine, under 5 months
366 Black Rex, Adult
367 Black Rex, under 5 months
368 Blue Rex, A.A.
369 Havana Rex, A.A.
370 Seal or Sable Rex, Adult
371 Seal or Sable Rex, under 5 months
372 Orange or Fawn Rex, Adult
373 Orange or Fawn Rex, under 5 months
374 A.O.V., Rex, A.A.
375 Rex Breeders, Adult (D)
376 Rex Breeders, under 5 months (D)
377 Rex Challenge, Adult (D)
378 Rex Challenge, under 5 months (D)
379 Gents' Exhibit, A.V., A.A. (D)
380 Ladies' Exhibit, A.V., A.A. (D)
381 A.V. Buck, A.A. (D)
382 A.V. Doe, A.A. (D)
383 Meat Rabbit, A.V., A.A. (M.D.)
384 Grand Challenge, A.A. (D)
385 LONDON CHAMPIONSHIP SHOW CLASS (D)
Entry Fee 10p. Prize Money £1, 50p, 25p, (donated). All receipts from Entry Fees will be given to the London Show without deduction. Please duplicate freely.

cannot enter, for there is a class called **Any Other Variety**. This is for all those breeds, which have not got their own classification. The only snag here is that there will be other breeds besides yours entered in the class. So you will be competing with other potential winners, if they had their own classes.

Do not forget, you must look for the **Any Other Variety** class in the Fancy section, because there will be one in the Fur and the Rex sections as well.

Next decide the amount of money that can be afforded to be spent. Then look at the **Duplicate** classes, to see what is on offer. Consider the quality of your exhibit and try to size up its chances and the possible opposition.

Red Eyed White, Adult.
Sable, Adult.
Black, Adult.
Agout/Chinchilla Adult.
Any Other Colour, Adult.

ANOTHER EXAMPLE
Red Eyed White, Adult.
Any Other Colour, Adult.
Red Eyed White, under 5 months.
Sable, under 5 months.
Black, under 5 months.
Agouti/Chinchilla, under 5 months.
Any Other Colour, under 5 months.

DUPLICATES

What are **Duplicates?** These are classes where different breeds compete together against each other. Deciding which ones offer yours the best chances only comes with experience.

There are a number of possible classes, not all will be found at every show. There is usually a **Breeders** and a **Challenge** in each section. That is *all breeds in that section* may compete. At the end comes the **Grand Challenge**, in which ALL breeds from *every* section may compete.

Many classes are obvious; e.g., *ladies* means the exhibit must belong to a lady. It may come from any section. *Gents* obviously is for those belonging to gentlemen only. **Bucks** and **Does** are also obvious. But some are not so simple. For example:

Novice The rabbit (not the exhibitor) must not have won a first or a Challenge Certificate in an Open Show.

Example of Entry Form

CITY OF PORTSMOUTH FANCIERS' SOCIETY

KNOWN AS
STRAIGHT
CLASS ↘

ALL LIVESTOCK & EGGS – ENTRY FORM

(ENTRY FEE FOR THIS SHOW 15p)(PER CLASS)

ANY OTHER CLASSES
↙KNOWN AS DUPLICATE
↙CLASSES

For Secretary's Use Only	Class No.	BREED & VARIETY	Ring No.	Sex	DUPLICATE CLASSES Entry Fee		Selling Price
	20	ADULT NETHERLAND DWARF WHITE	B.R.C 76 X01239	BUCK	29 (BREEDERS) 30 (CHALLENGE)	45p TOTAL	NOT FOR SALE
	24	NETHERLAND DWARF SABLE UNDER 5 MTS	B.R.C.77 X76542	DOE	35 (YOUNG BREEDERS) 36 (YOUNG CHALLENGE)		NOT FOR SALE
					52 (GRAND CHALLENGE) 60p		

I certify that the above are my own bona fide property at the time of entry, and agree to abide by the Rules.

Please state Specialist Clubs: -
NATIONAL NETH., DWARF CLUB
....
SOUTHERN NETH., DWARF CLUB
....
....
....

CASH ENCLOSED: -

For .7.... Entries @ 15p £1:05

For ...... Entries @ 10p £ : —

For ...... Entries @ 5p £ : —

£1:05

PAID

Membership Fee ....

OR MAYBE NOT?

NAME MR. HARRY WHATSIT ....
(Block letters)
ADDRESS 19 OAK TREE RD.
SOMEWHERE-ON-SEA
....
HANTS
....

Please state number of Rail Labels required:
(NOT REQUIRED
HAND STOCK)
....
....

Plate 8

Top: Mr. and Mrs. L. Cumberpatch's 8 weeks old Agouti Baby **"MUNCHA"** (showing the soft "nest" coat).

Bottom: K. Hird's Black Buck.

Limit Usually means that the rabbit has not won more than a stated number of firsts in Open Shows, usually three.

Star Shows Shows that are run under British Rabbit Council rules and awarding their Challenge Certificates. There are one star, two star, three star and five star status shows. This is that each Certificate won has the value of the number of stars shown on it. There are strict rules to be complied with by clubs applying to stage star shows. The more stars given, the more regulations and stipulations to be carried out.

Any Variety Any breed and any colour rabbit in the show may compete.

Novice Exhibitor The exhibitor is the novice and not necessarily the rabbit. He or she must not have won more than a stipulated number of firsts at Open shows.

Young Classes The exhibits must not exceed the age laid down by their breed clubs for a youngster. (This varies with the breeds). The Netherland Dwarf is the usual and most often found, five months. (It is, for example, under 4 months for Dutch babies.)

Young Stock Show This indicates that although there may be adult classes scheduled, the Challenge certificates are confined to the young classes only.

Adult Stock Show The other way round.

Open Show There are classes for both adult and young stock. It is open for anyone to compete, and the winning adult and winning youngster of each breed *must* be brought together to decide which one takes the Challenge Certificate.

Gift Classes This means that after the show, the rabbits will be sold for the benefit of the club, or some other cause.

Juvenile Classes Classes reserved for exhibits belonging to those between the ages of five and sixteen.

Any Age Explains itself.

Any Colour Explains itself.

CHOOSING WHICH CLASSES TO ENTER

Here you have to do a bit of guessing. Remember that a not so good specimen *may* come up in some classes, because the ones that beat it in its breed may not be entered in all duplicates. Weigh up possibilities and costs of fees.

Insecure method of holding.

CHAPTER 13

Odds And Ends

METHODS OF PICKING UP A RABBIT

A rabbit's ears are *not* for the purpose of picking it up. This is a particularly important rule for the Dwarf.

Place the hand under the rump to take the weight and put the other hand around the ears or under the belly to steady it. Never restrain a struggling rabbit by force. Release it, if it is on a table, or slacken the grip, if being held. Speak quietly and soothingly and begin again. Never frighten it. The aim must always be to gain its confidence.

INTERMEDIATE COAT

This is the coat that follows the nest, or baby coat. It will come through completely at about fourteen weeks and will last roughly from 2 - 4 weeks.

This is an ideal state for showing a youngster when an important show is on. The rabbit then goes into complete moult and will attain its full adult coat at a year onwards.

GESTATION PERIOD

This is the length of time an animal carries its young, in rabbits around 31 days, give or take a little either side.

COPOGRAPHY

This should not be confused with the eating of filth. The rabbit does not digest all its food completely at once. A certain amount passes through the gut, or intestines, without having been properly absorbed. This is passed out via the anus and is soft in consistency, as opposed to the normal hard pellets. The animal takes them direct from the anus and eats them, when the further digestion takes place.

SEXING

The testicles in the buck do not descend fully until it is several months old. To sex it, therefore, take the animal gently in the hand and hold upside down. Have an assistant if possible. Place the thumb near the sex orifice on the belly side and in between the back legs. Using either the index finger or the middle, whichever is most natural, place on the side of the orifice nearest the tail. Press the two fingers apart gently. This will stretch the orifice. If it remains round, press very slightly harder, the point of the penis should pop out in a buck. A long or oval shape is a doe.

MOULT

This is a perfectly normal procedure. It occurs at all kinds of times and for all kinds of reasons. It is simply the rabbit changing its coat.

The usual time for the adult to do this is once in autumn and again in spring. The autumn coat is slightly thicker.

Unfortunately, for show purposes, other things can contribute to premature moult. A spell of very hot weather can start it off. This is a hazard at Agricultural shows. Exhibits are in canvas marquees without much air circulating, so the heat is intensified.

Some judges are prepared to accept an exhibit with a little moult, regarding it as normal. Others will not tolerate it at all, as their opinion is that the animal is not in show condition. Both points of view are defensible. It is necessary to learn which judges hold which opinions for successful showing and in order not to waste money.

Correct way to lift a Dwarf

Lifting to display underside

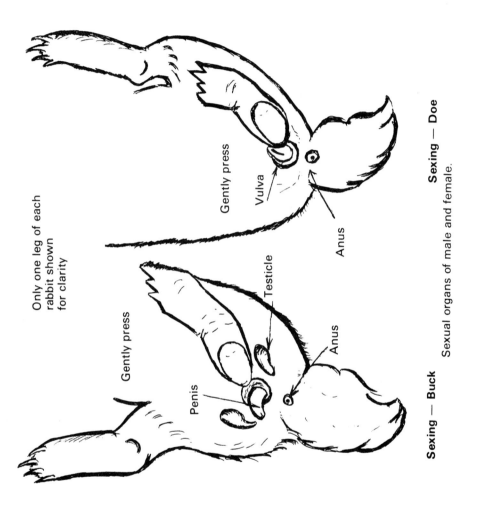

Only one leg of each rabbit shown for clarity

Gently press

Vulva

Anus

Gently press

Testicle

Penis

Anus

Sexing — Buck

Sexing — Doe

Sexual organs of male and female.

The Sexual Organs

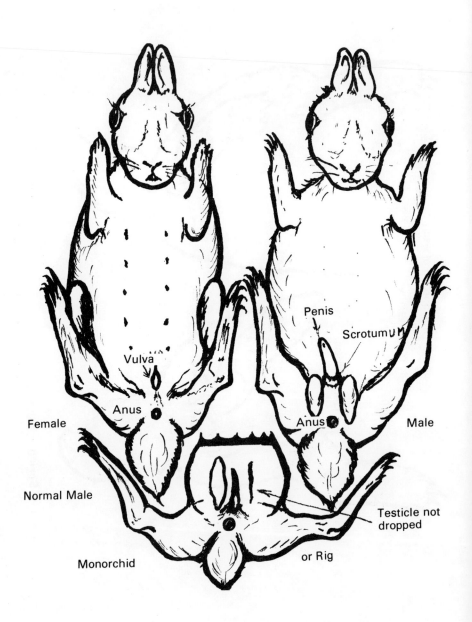

Penis

Scrotum

Vulva

Anus

Anus

Female

Male

Normal Male

Testicle not dropped

Monorchid

or Rig

CHAPTER 14

How To Reach The Top And Stay There

What divides the truly great Netherland Dwarf from the very good?
How does one produce it?

NECESSARY PERSONAL ATTRIBUTES

The first, middle and last requirements may be summed up by
ruthlessness, followed closely be the kind of patience usually found
only in the trainers of wild animals and show jumpers. This is a peculiar brand of patience, cultivated and nurtured, along with other
struggles, resulting in a kind of love-hate relationship existing all the
time.

The next requirement is the realisation that *the Dwarf is completely different from any other breed in almost every way*.

There is a common belief that the Dwarf is suitable for a child's
pet, held usually by those who have little or no knowledge of it. This
notion appears to be based on size. Would you, therefore, give a child
a ferret? It can be classed among the few top breeds totally *unsuitable*
for children until they have served an apprenticeship on easier breeds.

The Dwarf can be very nasty tempered, has small litters, reducing
the chances of producing a good show specimen, and the young often
do not survive. This is all very disheartening to an adult, let alone a
juvenile.

DEDICATION

Anyone who can stick to the first points, plus a few more, has a
good chance of breeding a truly great Dwarf. Many breeders slip back
after reaching the top, because they forget that cardinal rule, **Ruthlessness.**

ATTENTION TO STUDY

Study as many different animals from different breeders as possible. Study closely those that win consistently under Club Judges.

Specialist Clubs frequently have a non-breeders Panel also whose members have been selected because they enjoy the confidence of the breeders.

Try to pick out the style that belongs to the top studs. Try to get your stock from them.

This may be difficult. Don't judge too harshly and assume that a desire to help is absent. *Because* they are at the top, they are culling (weeding out, killing) possibly three quarters of what they breed. Because they can be trusted not to sell dud stock they often, genuinely, have nothing for sale.

Beware of those who *always* have stock available. Insist on seeing their rabbitries, if possible. There are, unfortunately, some breeders selling off stock that should be killed.

HOW TO PICK OUT LIKELY WINNERS

There is one foolproof method of selecting likely winners, barring unforeseen circumstances, that is peculiar to the Dwarf.

Look closely at four weeks old. That is the replica of what it will become. By six weeks, this may well have disappeared. Occasionally it lasts, or reappears a few weeks later, but not usually until about eight months. At three months it will probably look terrible. All the time keep firmly in mind what it looked like at a month.

After that, there are only two things, *standard* wise, to watch: **weight** and **ear length**. So long as it does not exceed 2 lbs in its young growing days, and the ears do not exceed 2 ins in length leave it alone, until it is about eight months old (apart from training, of course).

What must be realised and remembered is that in the Dwarf, the ears are fully grown at four months old; therefore, the body looks all out of proportion and the ears *appear* longer than they really are. Just keep measuring them. As long as they stay no more than 2 ins all is well. The body has a long way to go yet, and when it is fully mature, the ears will be just right.

The Dwarf is a slow maturing breed in every respect except for the ears and is not much use for show until about a year old. It will go on improving and has a long career ahead.

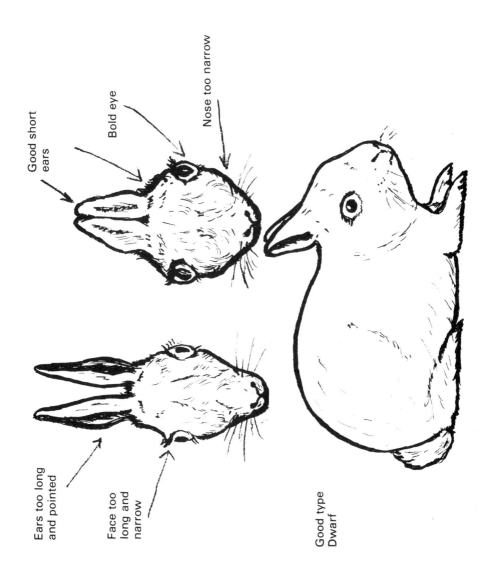

Good short
ears

Bold eye

Nose too narrow

Ears too long
and pointed

Face too
long and
narrow

Good type
Dwarf

WHAT IS RUTHLESSNESS?

Ruthlessness cannot be said too often. Discard, destroy rigidly, everything not up to your chosen set of rules. Don't be led astray because of other seemingly good points, particularly in a buck. Never mind if his ears are minute, rounded tips, erect, bullet head. If he has white armpits or pads, a narrow nose or skull, frosty nose, white hairs in ears, narrow shoulders — **out**. Discard him in favour of one with *adequate* attributes within the *standard* and with no disqualifications.

Faults once bred in from the buck's side are terribly difficult to eradicate, because all the does carry his blood.

RULES TO APPLY

Never use less than a top quality buck.
Never use two animals together carrying the same fault. (Do not forget to consult your records to see if a close relative carried one.)
Commit the *standard* to memory and apply it constantly.
Be Patient — endlessly.
Be Ruthless — absolutely.
Do Not Go Outside the Bloodline, unless you are looking for something special not already in the line. Then look for it in another breeder's stock that carries some of your blood. (It is wise to consult your original breeder about this, if possible, in early days.)

WHAT TO LOOK FOR IN THE BEST DWARF

Well set on **ears, short, erect, round tipped, well furred behind as well as in front.** (They need not be touching all the way up, but they show up to better advantage if they are.) No kinks or bends.

No **neck,** bullet **head** going straight back onto the shoulders. Turn the rabbit round with its rump towards you, for this gives an excellent view of this particular point which is easily missed from the front.

Bold eye, prominent and correct colour in both eyes.

Well rounded **haunches** well covered and plump, firm to the touch.

Cobby **body** alert and sitting close up, not flat out.

Not **overweight**.

148

SKILL

The skill is in doing what is required as it is important to remember that most points are given for type. It *must,* therefore, first and foremost be a *Dwarf.*

C. Graveling's English Dwarf (on the way).

CHAPTER 15

The Unstandardised Dwarf

The term 'unstandardised Dwarf' relates to any Dwarf or 'would be' Dwarf for which there is no *standard*. To understand the meaning, the fancier must go back a number of years, to when there was only a red-eyed white Dwarf.

INTRODUCTION OF COLOURS

Gradually, over a period of years, people began to breed colours. It took much patience and a long time before any of these could be recognised by the B.R.C. and granted a *standard*.

HOW A STANDARD IS GRANTED

The most important thing is to prove that any new breed, or new colour of an existing breed, breeds 'true'. It must breed true for *three* generations, and proof must be produced. In the days when the coloured Dwarfs were first becoming recognised, it was harder still, as it was then five generations.

The only exception is in the case of the Agouti, which is similar to the natural wild colour, and in itself it carries all the colours. Therefore from it can be obtained, eventually, almost any colour, when it is suitably mated and remated.

HOW A NEW COLOUR IS MADE

As previously described, the way a new colour is formed is either by taking the normal size breed and reducing it down, by systematic matings with true Dwarfs, until one has got the colour of the normal with the size and type of the Dwarf, *or*, if one wishes to produce a completely new colour, for which there is no normal size breed, by intermingling different colour Dwarfs, bearing in mind all the time, what colours are already present in the ancestry of each. Hence the necessity of complete and accurate records.

As the Agouti carries all colours, this is one used a great deal for making new colours. It can take many years to produce a new true breeding colour.

FOR AND AGAINST

There are some who say there are already too many colours in existence. However, one also has to bear in mind, those interested in either 'dwarfing' a breed or producing another colour and, therefore, pursue a course of introducing new types.

Without the earlier experimenters, the curious, the geneticists, there would be no progress, and certainly many of our now well established and very beautiful colours would never have come into being. Who can say what other wonderful or beautiful things there are waiting to be discovered? In the Netherland Dwarf breed it can truly be said there is room for everyone to his own tastes.

B.R.C. RULES GOVERNING ALTERATIONS TO STANDARDS

The B.R.C. publish a new *Standards* book only once every five years. No alterations relating to disqualifications, colours, faults or anything of that nature can be accepted until the next five year period.

There is a sound reason for this. Judges must judge to the standards laid down in this book for the following reasons:

1. If Breed Clubs could alter their rules at any time.

2. Or new colours or breeds are introduced arbitrarily it would be impossible for judges to keep pace with them. Also, all kinds of possibly undesirable elements, detrimental to breeds and the Fancy in general could creep in.

It is unfortunate if a colour becomes true breeding in the middle of this cycle, but worse if it happens in the first or second year. But it must be seen to anyone with the welfare of the Fancy at heart, that the rule is a good and necessary one.

How This Affects The Netherland Dwarf

People experimenting with new colours found it very difficult to continue. Some become disheartened, and some gave up trying as there was no way and nowhere to show their stock. Nor could they establish how far along the road they had got. (This only applies to the Dwarf, remember, as it was still a very new breed in those days.) Colours were few in number and confined only to the very straightforward ones, such as Blacks, Sables and Smoke Pearls.

It would have been a pity, if those early pioneers had been lost to the Dwarf Fancy. We should undoubtedly have lost (or never seen) some of today's most beautiful colours.

ORIGIN OF THE UNSTANDARDISED CLASS

The National Dwarf Club committee began some serious thinking. Ideas were put forward, discussed, abandoned, postponed and, eventually, the committee came up with the idea of a class for 'unstandardised' colours. In this could be entered anything that was reasonably 'on the way'. This is not to say that just any old thing resembling a dwarf type and weighing as much as 4 lbs. could be entered. It was intended for the serious breeder, who was getting somewhere near in size and colour and beginning to show the dwarf type.

One of the first to be shown officially in this was a Himalayan, weighing 3¼ lbs. which had quite a reasonable type and ears, measuring only 2½ ins. It was bred by a man living on the south coast, who died suddenly, before he could get any further with it. Fortunately, his stock was taken over by an enthusiast and today, the Himalayan Dwarf is a very attractive addition and, curiously enough, usually very small.

APPROACH TO THE B.R.C.

The B.R.C. was approached for permission for this class. They refused for any open shows run under B.R.C. rules, as it could have opened the way to all kinds of requests from other breeds.

However, they said that there was nothing to prevent the Netherland Dwarf Club from putting on such a class at its own *breed specialist* shows.

A B.R.C. Challenge certificate could not be given for the class, of course; and it must be confined to all Dwarf breed Shows alone, where no other breeds were competing.

OPENING FOR EXPERIMENTALISTS

This proposal proved an excellent solution. First the National and then the various Area Dwarf clubs began including this class in their **Young Stock** and **Adult Stock** Shows. Breeders were now able to show what they were breeding, and could see how much progress had been made, discuss problems with other breeders and even recruit other interested breeders.

There are many names associated with the production of different colours and it would be invidious to mention some without mentioning all, but we should never forget the debt we owe them, for their work and fight in the early days.

MARKED SPECIMENS

The Unstandardised class has encouraged a great upsurge of enthusiasm in the middle 1970's to 'Dwarf' some of the 'marked' breeds. The Dutch and English pattern are on the way, and the Otter is just about there. They will probably appear in the 1980 *Standards* book. This is the next time any new colours can be registered. Obviously, it will be very interesting to see what has arrived. This 'Unstandardised' class still exists today at the all Dwarf Stock shows.

CHAPTER 16

Wildfood and Greenfood From the Garden (Netherland Dwarf Only)

This chapter applies only to the Netherland Dwarf. There are many other wildfoods suitable for rabbits of a bigger breed; e.g. Docks, and this is not, also, a complete list. However, it should provide sufficient guidance for the beginner to use for a considerable time, until he has got plenty of experience and has talked to a number of breeders.

Make the best of what is available cheaply. There is much here that can be used, even by the non-greens feeders. In fact, there are some things that should be in the 'larder' of *all* breeders, whatever they feed.

HAY

Most people can make some kind of hay, whether they live in towns or country. When mowing the lawn do not use it all for compost. Layer some over the newly cut lawn and leave it to dry. Gather up at night and put somewhere safe from rain (or cover it with a waterproof covering). Spread it out again the next day. Continue like this until it is quite dry, turning it over with a fork to keep the air circulating.

NETTLES

Nettles are excellent food, but they must not be fed fresh. Nettle hay is one of the most nourishing foods. You make it in exactly the same way as ordinary hay. Simply put on thick gloves and scythe it down, then continue as usual.

155

PERMITTED FOODS

In the following lists, there are a number of wild flowers, etc., all of which are good to mix in with your home made hay. There are also a number of things which must **never** be fed:

Never feed anything grown from a bulb.

Never feed any evergreen.

Do not feed berries.

Ivy and Rhubarb leaves are **not** safe for Dwarfs, although they may be fed under certain conditions to larger breeds.

REASONS FOR STUDY

A fancier should be able to distinguish some of the wild flowers and herbs, even if pellet feeding and water are customary. There are so many with medicinal qualities that will be required from time to time, when illness strikes, that an understanding of what properties each possesses and the ability to recognise them is vital.

Many will be completely familiar by sight; but this, in itself, is not sufficient. It is necessary to know which are dangerous and which are beneficial, and for what purposes, if you are not to kill your stock, unwittingly, and also to get the best value from green food.

Because a number of plants are 'killers' and some very difficult to distinguish from 'beneficial', this chapter will contain more pictures than writing, so that you can study and familiarise yourself with the most common ones.

UNDERSTANDING VITAL

Take the first two pictures together, they are **killers**, the **Deadly Night Shade** and the **Woody Night Shade**. Learn them well and make sure you know them.

Six To Study Together

Next in importance come six rather similar at a casual glance, four are excellent, but the other two are killers.

First, the killers:

Hemlock Note the wispy *foliage* and the smooth, dark spotted stems that will give this one away.

Fools' Parsley Flowers in July and August and has a particularly evil smell.

156

Now the four first class feeds (**not harmful**):

Hedge Parsley Especially good and one of the earliest to appear in the year, early June and continues well into September. Has a grooved stem.

Cow Parsley Feed this while it is young. An excellent food. Be careful not to overdo the quantity because it is a laxative. Very much enjoyed.

Shepherd's Purse Absolutely invaluable both as a food and a medicine. Can be fed fresh or dried. Used against Scours. Gather as much as possible; dry off, store for winter use for Scours or Diarrhoea. Flowers throughout the summer.

Wild Carrot (or garden carrot leafy tops) Much enjoyed. If the leafy end of a carrot is cut off and placed in a saucer of water it will quickly produce leaf so the supply can be kept going. Wild variety: May to August.

ASTRINGENTS

(For use against Scours and Diarrhoea)

Next in importance, perhaps, are the astringent plants. They are likely to be required on numerous occasions as, if fed quickly enough, they can stop the trouble at its onset — unless it is a sign of something more deep seated.

Shepherd's Purse Has already been described in some detail; it is one of the best.

Strawberry and Raspberry Leaves These are excellent but not always procurable. **Bramble Leaves** are the next best thing and are available in quantity over a long period (June to September). Can be dried, also. Not everyone is familiar with the leaf.

Don't forget the little wild strawberry which is exactly like a miniature strawberry and flowers throughout the summer.

Goosegrass Must be fed fresh. June and July.

Agrimony and Avens Both have yellow flowers and bloom in June and July. Both must be fed fresh. Both come under the heading of Tonics, also.

Burnet Very distinctive flowers, found almost everywhere. Leaves have a distinct cucumber smell. Often used in salads. Often called the Salad Burnet. Flowers June to September.

Herb Robert This is an excellent normal food as well.

Note A good supply of this group dried off should be adequate for winter requirements for Scours and Diarrhoea.

157

LAXATIVES

These will not be necessary as frequently as the astringents, but should always be available. **Clovers** are a subject of much debate, discussed later in the chapter.

Chickweed This is very laxative, so be careful, as it is much liked. Use it in a mixed feed with others. Add a little more of it, if being used for constipation. Do not confuse it with the Scarlet Pimpernel — Chickweed has **white** flowers. Chickweed will flower from April right on through the autumn. Scarlet Pimpernel from May to November, so it can be difficult. Remember the colour.

Dandelion Leaves and flowers can be fed. Not too much at a time for a Dwarf, preferably in a mixed feed.

Groundsel Very useful indeed, as it can be found the whole year round, and is also found in gardens. It is also used to help through the moult. Rabbits love it.

Hogweed This has a thick, grooved and hairy stem, which is hollow. It is in flower — white to pinky white — from June to September. It is very good indeed added to a mixed bunch.

Hawkbit or Hawkweed This is better avoided for Dwarfs. There are several varieties, some are astringent and some laxative. Because of the size of the Dwarf, it would be absolutely vital to know which was which. Its stem is tough and its leaves wither quickly. The flowers are yellow.

Sow Thistle This is perfectly safe to feed alone, and is very much liked. Flowers from August to September. A good, safe laxative. Excellent in a mixed bunch also.

MOULT

Some wild foods are very helpful in getting rabbits through the moult, particularly any that may be 'stuck' in the process. **Groundsel**, pictured and described under Laxatives, is excellent, as is **Garden Parsley**.

GENERAL TONICS

General tonic food is useful to know and is as follows:

Agrimony Also an astringent. (See under that category.) Can be fed to adults or youngsters.

Coltsfoot Very useful as it flowers as early as March. Single yellow flowers appearing before the leaves. Will often tempt a 'poor' appetite. Rabbits suffering from chills will often take some.

Comfrey Very good food indeed, both as a tonic and for general digestive upsets. Use it with 'off colour' animals. Can be white, pink or purple according to the part of the country in which it is found.

Watercress This is best fed crushed. The wild variety can be found near water from May to October and is general to the British Isles.

ALL ROUND FOOD MIXTURES

Greenstuff which may be used with others are as follows:

Clover The Clover family was considered doubtful some years ago as there are so many varieties, not all of them safe. Opinions have altered considerably recently, so it is up to you to decide for yourself.

The Clovers belong to the Vetch and Trefoil family, *Leguminosae*, and as these are splendid foods it is difficult to see why the Clovers should be excluded. It may be because they are highly laxative and should be fed *only* in small quantities among a generous mixture of others. For the Dwarf, therefore, it might be wiser to leave them alone at first.

Trefoils Very safe and found in large variety. The most common is Birds' Foot Trefoil, often known as Lady's Slipper. It is found from June to October and is very popular with farmers, as it makes excellent hay in with other mixtures.

Vetches This consists of a very large family and, taking all varieties into consideration, will give a season from May to September. It comes in many colours and grows in dry, stony, rocky or chalky soils. It is a first class food and should form a part of any dried hay mixture, along with grass cuttings, nettles, etc. Sainfoin variety is probably one of the best.

Heathers All the heathers are safe and some kinds can be found most of the year round. *Ling* is found almost everywhere, and although officially it flowers June to September, the flowers can be found in varying stages of fading for almost nine months. The *Erica tetralix* is much enjoyed, as it is sweet to the taste.

Thistle Family Remember the Sow Thistle is also a laxative. All other thistles are a good mixed bunch with others. Be sure they are thoroughly dried, because as such they are good for hay making.

159

They can be found in different varieties from June to October.
Ground Elder The curse of the gardener! Very useful as it can be found from April to October.
Yarrow One of the most common wild flowers from June to the end of the year. Very good food and very distinctive.
Plantain This is useful because it has a long season, but not of any great food value. Can be used when others are in short supply. The stem is too stiff and coarse for Dwarfs, so strip flowers and leaves off.

LEARN THESE VERY CAREFULLY, THEY ARE EXTREMELY DANGEROUS

Bindweed Can be found in fields and gardens.
Convolvulus Can be found in fields and gardens.
Dog Mercury Fields and ditches.
Foxglove Both wild and garden varieties. June to September.
Kingcup Very poisonous indeed. Found in marshy, wet places. March to August.
Spurge Frequently found in gardens. Stem contains a milky white substance and is very dangerous.

A NEWCOMER TO THE RABBIT WORLD

Lucerne Although this has long been known on the Continent and in Great Britain for the feeding of larger farm animals, it is only during the last few years that it has really taken hold in the rabbit world. Yet it will probably become one of the best and most useful of feeds.

Fed green it is absolutely marvellous as well as being suitable for drying into hay for winter use, crammed full of nourishment. If you have some spare part of your garden or allotment, plant it and this will more than repay for the ground it takes up. Feed flowers and leaves, the flowers in the wild state from May to July.

It has been grown in England for many years for ploughing back into the land, so nutritious was it thought to be. Experiments are taking place now to product a lucerne pellet.

GARDEN GREENS AND CULTIVATED FOOD

We must not forget that many of the everyday vegetables and

flowers in gardens have high food content. Below is a list of those to feed and those to avoid. Some come into the category of both wild and cultivated.

Good

Brussels Sprouts (only about one for Dwarfs).

Broccoli.

Beans, green (avoid leaves for Dwarfs).

Carrot (root and leaf).

Chives (green stems only).

Celery (stalks and tops).

Cabbage (feed this with great discretion to Dwarfs, only very small quantity. Very, very laxative and makes urine smell strong).

Cauliflower (any part. A small piece of stump is much enjoyed).

Chicory (Excellent. Another one worth finding a small place for in garden).

Fennel (A herb used in cooking).

Kale (Stalk and leaf).

Peas (Shucks and haulms as well. Haulms dry excellently for winter use).

Potato Peelings (Well washed and dried, or damp. Good for nursing does).

Spinach (rich in iron). An 'off colour' rabbit will sometimes fancy a leaf.

Swede (small portion).

This by no means exhausts the list, but is a rough guide of what is most commonly available in a garden and suitable for Dwarfs.

Never Feed

Buttercup.

Bindweed.

Berries.

Bulbs (any form).

Celandine.

Cowslip.

Ferns.

Geranium (garden variety).

Holly.

Ivy.

Laburnum.

Lettuce. This is a controversial green. It should never be fed in quantity, and a Dwarf is better without it.

Mistletoe.

Groundsel   Shepherds purse

Privet.
Potato Tops (**very** dangerous).
Tomato (leaves and stalks).

Talk to the old experienced fanciers as much as possible. They will teach you a great deal about the feeding of greenstuff; but, one warning, make sure they are Dwarf breeders, because, as said before, there are many plants suitable for larger breeds that would kill a Dwarf.

If in doubt, *do not feed*. If a new plant try only a *small* piece at first.

CHAPTER 17

The Dwarf Lop

Strictly speaking, the Dwarf Lop does not belong to the Netherland Dwarf family. It is, indeed, possible that the Dwarf part of the name may be changed at some future time.

All the coloured Netherland Dwarfs have been bred down over a period of years from their full size counterparts (normal breeds), as has the Dwarf Lop, but there the similarity ends. There are essential differences.

ORIGINS OF THE NETHERLAND DWARF

Think back how the original Red Eyed White Dwarf came about. It was a 'sport', a mutation, a freak, which was then cultivated and which bore no resemblance to its early parentage. There were only red eyed white Dwarfs at first. It is important to remember this, if one is to understand the difference.

ORIGIN OF THE COLOURS

It was only later, after true breeding red eyed whites was well established, that anyone thought of producing a coloured one.

The red eyed white was mated with some of the larger normal breeds (usually fur breeds). The Smoke Pearl and the Sable were great favourites. It was only the colour that was wanted. Essentially the SHAPE was to be that of the Dwarf. It took years to get the coloured Netherland Dwarf size type and true colour.

In the early generations of cross breeding, fanciers lost *colour* from the normal breed and *type* from the Dwarf. Only by continual breeding and inbreeding and with much perseverance did the Nether-

163

Lopped ears of French Lop, with dwarfed size, but still twice that of Netherland Dwarf. (Desired weight 4lbs. 4oz.)

Erect ears and size of Netherland Dwarf. (Desired weight 2lbs. 2oz.)

Dwarf French Lop

land Dwarf type emerge with the normal breeds' colours. Then more years elapsed before anyone could claim to breed them true.

ORIGIN OF DWARF LOP

The Dwarf Lop, however, is completely the other way round. Admittedly the French Lop and a 'dwarf type breed' were used; *but* the idea was to get the type and shape of the big French Lop in a Dwarf size which is not the same thing at all. In Holland it took 17 years to produce what was wanted.

Essentially, the coloured Netherland Dwarf is a Dwarf in type, whatever its colour. The Dwarf Lop is a Lop in type and a Dwarf in size.

165

Index

Enteritis, 119
Expense, 2, 4
Eyes, 28, 65
  diseases and injuries, 97, 109, 114, 116, 118
  insertion of drops, 106-8, 118

Faeces, 98
  impaction, 119
Faults, 30, 32-3, 35, 53, 65, 148
Fawn, 62
Feeding
  coccidiostats, 50-1, 110
  copography, 139-40
  costs, 2, 4
  for breeding does, 24, 25
  for bucks, 24-5
  for pregnant does, 45
  methods, 19-25
  of weaned young, 48
  while travelling, 74
  see also Greenfood; Wildfood
First aid equipment, 129-30
Fits, see Convulsions
Foundation stock, 27

Genetics, xi, 53
Gestation period, 41, 139
Greenfood, 21-2, 155-62

Handling, 80
  method of lifting, 139, 141
Hay, 24, 155
Hayracks, 23
Health, 97-100
Heat exhaustion, 118-19
  see also Overheating
Himalayan, 62, 63, 153
Hutches, 7-18
  cleaning after coccidiosis, 51, 112
  cleaning tools, 18
  creosoting or painting, 122
  for does with litters, 39
  positioning, 12, 16
  space required, 2, 7
Hygiene
  hutch cleaning tools, 18
  of doe with litter, 51

Injuries, 119-20

Judges, 131

Killing, 111, 113

Laxatives, 158
Lilacs, 60

Mash, 24
Mating, 39, 41-3
  programmes, 52
  records, 91
Moult, 60, 99-100, 140, 158
Myxomatosis, 120-1

National Netherland Dwarf Club, 95, 153-4
Nest boxes, 46, 47
Nesting, 41, 45, 47
Noses, 28
  'frosty' or 'putty', 58

Oats, 21
Opals, 61
Orange, 62
Origins of breed, x
Otter, pattern, 154
Overheating, 105
  see also Heat exhaustion

Paralysis, 122-4
Pellets (droppings), see Faeces
Pellets (feed), 19, 22
Pneumonia, 121
Poisoning, 121-2
Poisonous plants, 156, 160, 161

Rearing, 45-8
Recessive genes, 53
Record keeping, x, 54, 88-91
  use of rings, 86, 88
Red water (urinary disorder), 125
Ringing, 36-8, 85-91, 93

Sables, 53-4, 57
Sawdust, 7, 70
Schedules, 133-7
Scours (diarrhoea), 125-6
  homemade mixture, 130
Seal point, 64
Sexing, 140, 143-4
Sexual organs, 97
  of breeding doe, 30
  of stud buck, 28
  vent disease, 128

Shows
  advantages of Dwarfs, 132
  entries, 76, 78, 132
  hints on entering, 131-7
  incidence of disease, 102
  picking likely winners, 146, 148
  preparation, 69-82
  schedules, 133-7
  star grading, 94
  transporting stock, 133
  travelling costs, 4
Shutters, 9
Size of Dwarf, 1, 3, 5
Smoke Pearls, 53-4
Snuffles, 105, 126-7
Squirrel, 54, 60
Standard, 34, 65-8
  introduction of colours, 151-2
  rules governing alterations, 152-3
Steel, 62, 64
Sticky eye, 109
Stock selection and acquisition, 27-38
Suckling, 47
Sunlight, exposure to, 9

Teeth, 98-9
  disorders, 127

Ticking, 57
Toe-nails, 74
  cutting, 115, 117, 127-8
Tonics, 158-9
Tortoiseshells, 55, 61-2
Training, 1, 75, 77, 80-3
  to use water bottles, 21
Transfer of stock, 36, 93
Travelling boxes, 74, 76

Unstandardised colours, 64, 151-4
Urinary tract infection, 125

Vent disease, 128
Viciousness, 82

Washing, 69-70
Water, 20, 21
Waterproofing, 12
Weaning, 47
Weight, 28, 65, 146
'Wet eye', 97
Whites, 55
  cleaning, 69-70, 72
  for foundation stock, 27
Wildfood, 155-62
Worms, 129